THE LITTLE BOOK

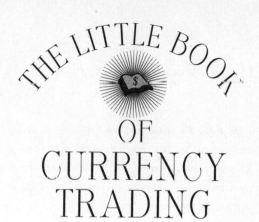

OF
CURRENCY
TRADING

Little Book Big Profits Series

In the *Little Book Big Profits* series, the brightest icons in the financial world write on topics that range from tried-and-true investment strategies to tomorrow's new trends. Each book offers a unique perspective on investing, allowing the reader to pick and choose from the very best in investment advice today.

Books in the *Little Book Big Profits* series include:

THE LITTLE BOOK

OF

CURRENCY
TRADING

*How to Make Big Profits in
the World of Forex*

KATHY LIEN

WILEY

John Wiley & Sons, Inc.

Published by John Wiley & Sons, Inc., Hoboken, New Jersey.
Published simultaneously in Canada.

For general information on our other products and services or for technical support, please contact our
Customer Care Department within the United States at (800) 762-2974, outside the United States at
(317) 572-3993 or fax (317) 572-4002.

Wiley also publishes its books in a variety of electronic formats. Some content that appears in print
may not be available in electronic books. For more information about Wiley products, visit our web site
at www.wiley.com.

ISBN 978-0-470-77035-1 (cloth); 978-1-118-01841-5 (ebk); 978-1-118-01840-8 (ebk);
978-1-118-01839-2 (ebk)

Printed in the United States of America
10 9 8 7 6 5 4 3 2 1

To my family, loved ones, and all of those
who have inspired me!

Contents

Introduction

— ∾ —

I HAVE ALWAYS CONSIDERED MYSELF LUCKY. When I was 10 years old, my mother's favorite performer from Hong Kong was doing a retirement concert in Atlantic City. The concert hall was packed with what must have been more than 1,000 people. When we took our seats, the performer told us that there would be a surprise giveaway of memorabilia from her past performances. When I was picked, I screamed in delight at winning a gorgeous antique watch. A few years later, I won a sweepstakes for a free Hawaiian vacation. I graduated college when I was just 18 years old, landed one of the first jobs that I've ever interviewed for, got out of the stock market before the technology bubble burst, met the man of my dreams at 23, and was never at risk of losing my job during the global financial crisis.

Lady Luck has certainly smiled on me and I won't take her for granted, but being lucky was not the only thing that got me where I am today. I doubt that New York University's Stern School of Business would have let me graduate college at an age when most people graduate high school just because of luck. Being smart, having a strong work ethic, recognizing opportunities when they appear, and knowing how to grab them is just as important as being lucky. In other words, luck needs to be combined with skill.

Over the past few years, we've all had to deal with financial crises. A lot of people lost their shirts and many are still struggling to recover. Those who survived without great loss are lucky. But should we be content with just being lucky? After all, some people not only survived but thrived during the financial crisis. When a crisis hits, you can sit back and watch in shock as your money evaporates or you can go on the offensive and take advantage of the opportunities in front of you. The key is to recognize those opportunities and know how to act on them when they appear.

One increasingly popular way of capitalizing on the up and down movements in the financial markets is through currencies. Between 2004 and 2010, the daily turnover or volume in the forex market more than doubled from $1.9 trillion to $4 trillion. Before the technology boom, investing and trading in the forex market was limited to institutional investors, hedge funds, and other deep-pocketed players. However, that changed when foreign exchange brokers brought their platforms online and made the market available to individual traders. Since then the number of people trading forex has exploded and it is only expected to grow. Many people have already discovered forex trading—it may be time for you to learn why the market has become so popular, too.

Foreign exchange movements touch everyone's lives in one way or another. Whether you've traded forex before or not, you've bought and sold currencies. If you've traveled abroad or bought something on eBay from a seller in another country, that counts! Or if you are a small-business owner, you trade forex when you buy and sell products imported from other countries.

Maybe you think you're exempt from needing to know about forex trading because you invest solely in U.S. stocks. But that's not true anymore. If the companies you invest in have any foreign operations or payables and receivables in different currencies, you're still exposed to currency risk. As a result, it is important for any trader or investor to stay on top of exchange rates and to know how much currencies are worth.

Of course, the sharp increase in foreign exchange trading activity is not just due to people following currencies.

Investors and traders are participating in the market for speculation, hedging, investment, and other transactional purposes.

There are many different ways to trade currencies; one of the best ways to get started is to trade what you know. Big stories and headlines in the financial markets that affect equities will generally affect currencies. So if you hear a story that is bad for a country's economy or gives foreign investors cause to be nervous, then there is a chance that investors will panic and bail out of the currency. When people panic, they always sell first and ask questions later. If the news is significant enough, it might also have a lasting impact on the currency. *The Little Book of Currency Trading* is dedicated to teaching you some skillful ways of turning headlines into trading opportunities.

Currencies can also move in one direction for a very long time; this book will illustrate ways to find opportunities to join the trend and when to pick tops and bottoms using a trading tool that I developed that clearly indicates whether a currency is in a trend or range. More seasoned traders will know that skillfully managing the trade is just as important as finding a good place to enter, so we'll spend time talking about how to bag the winners.

The forex market also has many unique characteristics that can make it riskier than other markets. I will show you how to manage the risk and how to find the best trades. Relying solely on luck can be dangerous and therefore I strongly believe that everyone should only take trades that are supported by as many variables as possible. The secret to being successful in currency trading and life is to take things seriously—treat your trading like a business and not a recreational hobby. It takes practice to really learn how to trade currencies well, and having a strong work ethic will help.

With knowledge of the market, a good strategy, solid money management, and a little bit of luck, you will be on your way to thriving in the forex market.

THE LITTLE BOOK

OF
CURRENCY
TRADING

Chapter One

When Lightning Strikes

Financial Crises and the Rise of Currency Trading

DO YOU KNOW SOMEONE WHO'S BEEN STRUCK BY LIGHTNING? What about someone who's been struck by lightning *twice*? According to the National Weather Service, the odds of someone being struck by lightning in a given year are 1 in 750,000. That makes it extremely unlikely that a person will be struck by lightning once, much less twice.

However, because lightning aims for the tallest object in a given area, it's not at all uncommon for it to hit the same place more than once. For that reason, lightning rods are placed atop city skyscrapers to attract the bolts and absorb the hit.

Lightning rods attract lightning just like financial markets attract greed, which inevitably brews disaster. Given the right conditions, disasters in the financial markets—like lightning—can hit more than once and investors must be prepared.

Back in 2007, Nassim Nicholas Taleb wrote what became a very famous book called *The Black Swan: The Impact of the Highly Improbable*. Taleb describes a Black Swan as an extremely rare event that catches people by surprise, has a major impact, and is then rationalized as if it had been expected to happen all along. Unfortunately, as we've all seen, Black Swan events have become much more common in recent years. As bubbles in the economy begin to reach their breaking points, it is important for investors to identify ways to deflect risk and possibly capitalize on those events because fortunes are at stake. In fact, two of the world's most famous global investors made their fortunes when other people were panicking and running for the exit.

In 1992, at the ripe young age of 62, George Soros gambled that the U.K. would not be able to maintain high interest rates necessary to keep the British pound within the tight currency band mandated by Exchange Rate Mechanism (ERM). Soros believed the weak economy and high unemployment would force the U.K. to abandon the ERM and cut rates. He turned his speculation into action by establishing a massive $10 billion short position in the British pound through the use of as many different instruments as he could find. Of course, Soros was not the only one selling the pound. As speculation grew about the U.K. abandoning the ERM, no one wanted to hold pounds. What separated Soros from other investors was that when most people were on the defensive, selling pounds and squaring their exposures into the madness, Soros was on the offensive, attacking the pound until the Bank of England cried uncle. A month later, Soros's Quantum Fund cashed in and banked approximately $2 billion in profit.

The second financial legend is Sir John Templeton, who took a very different approach from that of George Soros. Founder of the world's largest equity fund, the Templeton Growth Fund, Templeton was a deeply religious man and a contrarian at heart. He loved to buy the crashes and come in during what he called times of "maximum pessimism." For example, Templeton swooped into Ford when the automaker appeared to be headed for bankruptcy in 1978 and poured money into Peru when it was awash with communists in the 1980s. However, he was not always a buyer. In 2000, when everyone else was buying technology stocks, he shorted dozens of technology companies. Templeton liked to get in when the underlying fundamentals were extremely out of line with the perceptions of the reality. Those opportunities don't come along every day, but when they do, they can present enormous opportunities.

The Worst Decade Ever

Time magazine labeled the first 10 years of the twenty-first century as the worst decade ever. Apart from wars and environmental catastrophes, there were two market crashes: the dot-com bubble at the beginning of the decade and the global financial crisis at the end. The global financial crisis wiped out the savings of families around the world, plunged millions of people into unemployment, and claimed a number of Wall Street's oldest institutions including Lehman Brothers, Merrill Lynch, and Bear Stearns. Most people did not imagine that a company like Lehman, that was established in 1850 and survived two World Wars and the Great Depression, could be pushed into bankruptcy during our lifetime. There are countless stories of individual investors who lost 50 to 90 percent of their retirement funds. The debacle in one way or another affected the lives of every American. Yet, believe it or not, a handful of savvy investors profited handsomely during this period when most were losing their shirts.

The subprime crisis that began in 2007 eventually morphed into the global financial crisis. The origin of the crisis was the popping of the technology bubble, which led Alan Greenspan, the Federal Reserve chairman at the time, to stimulate the economy by cutting interest rates aggressively. Unfortunately, he left interest rates too low for too long, creating housing and credit bubbles. Money was flowing into the U.S. economy from spigots as the Dow Jones Industrial Average raced from 8,000 in 2003 to a high 14,000 by 2007. The low cost of borrowing encouraged Americans to refinance their current homes, trade up, or buy investment property—and in some cases, all of the above.

Many of you may have participated or at least had ringside seats to the hysteria—even if it was only watching TV shows like *Flip This House* on A&E or *Flip That House* on the Discovery Channel. At the time, everyone from your local barber to taxi drivers was dabbling in real estate and believed to the core that in the long term, you could never lose money on housing. Boy, were they wrong. By 2005, real estate had accounted for 70 percent of the rise in net household wealth and an astounding 50 percent of overall growth in the U.S. economy in the first half of that year. Between 2001 and 2005, more than half of the private sector payroll jobs created were in housing related sectors. Who could blame the average American when house prices in places like Phoenix, Arizona, were rising as much as 45 percent a quarter. But when things got bad, they became very bad very quickly. When the housing bubble burst, prices in some states fell nearly 50 percent from their peak levels in 2006. Between the middle of 2007 and the beginning of 2009, U.S. stocks also dropped more than 50 percent. By March 2009, Americans lost more than $15 trillion in total net worth. The housing market bubble is exactly what Sir John Templeton would have called "maximum optimism."

In retrospect, many of us would wonder, how could we have not seen the warnings signs. With banks willing to lend to almost anyone, and average Americans overloading on debt, how could it have gone on forever? At the time, the bursting of the technology bubble was still in recent memory, which should have reminded us about the consequences of excesses. Although the subprime crisis created the largest housing bubble ever, it was certainly not the only one in recent history.

In the past 40 years alone, there were two housing bubbles in the United States, one that peaked in 1979 and another in 1989. Between 1987 and 1991, the housing bubble in Japan also collapsed, pushing the country into a long period of zero growth and what the Japanese referred to as the "Lost Decade." In 1998, the housing market in Hong Kong collapsed after the central bank raised interest rates from 8 to 23 percent to defend the currency during the Asian financial crisis. These bubbles may have occurred outside U.S. borders but they had global ramifications and made headlines across the world. Unfortunately, most U.S. homeowners and investors missed these all-too-obvious warning signs.

In fairness, a small number of experts, including Templeton just before he passed away, warned that the bubble would eventually burst, but their contrarian views were written off and fell on deaf ears. The crisis wiped out individual investors, mutual funds, hedge funds, and investments banks, but for those who anticipated the collapse, knew that bubbles eventually become deflated, and took speculative positions, fortunes were made. The biggest winner that we know of was John Paulson of Paulson & Company. The soft-spoken Harvard MBA and hedge fund manager was convinced that subprime mortgages would falter and began to warn his investors in 2006 that the housing bubble was bound to pop. His hedge fund made significant bets in anticipation of a collapse and by September 2007, his funds were up an average of 340 percent.

At a time when almost everyone else was losing money, Paulson and his investors raked in billions. In performance fees alone, Paulson's nine funds earned more than $2.5 billion between September 2006 and September 2007. Other winners in this period included Philip Falcone of Harbinger Capital Partners and Jim Simons of Renaissance Technologies LLC, both of whom collected more than $1 billion in performance fees, with Simons's $6 billion Medallion fund returning more than 50 percent. While all three of these funds bet successfully on the collapse in the housing market, other market players found alternative paths to making money from the subprime crisis.

Citadel Investment Group, one of the world's largest hedge funds, returned more than $800 million by purchasing distressed debt that no one else was willing to buy. For example, they took over the energy trades of Amaranth Advisors and acquired stakes in companies such as E*Trade.

Finally, the third set of funds that made money during the subprime crisis were high frequency trading outfits that focused on ultra short-term trading opportunities. Focusing on the very short term made them less exposed to the big moves in the market. Contrary to popular belief, the subprime crisis did not produce just losers, particularly among those who anticipated the crisis, picked up bargains, or focused on very short-term opportunities.

The Eurozone Feels the Squeeze

One crisis has led to another and now we are faced with new troubles in Europe. In response to the global financial crisis, central banks around the world increased spending to stimulate their economies and as a result drove their fiscal deficits to double-digit levels. Although many countries, including the United States and the United Kingdom, also have heavy debt burdens as a percentage of GDP, the Eurozone was punished when news broke that Greece's budget deficit, at 13 percent of GDP, was twice as large as previously estimated. They had fudged the numbers and were forced to admit the real state of their finances.

This triggered a series of warnings and then downgrades by rating agencies as investors grew concerned about the country's high borrowing costs and ability to meet upcoming debt payments. European policy makers let the problems exacerbate, to the criticism of many investors, before finally stepping in with a massive rescue plan that was worth nearly USD$1 trillion. Unfortunately, the ambitious plan failed to stabilize the markets even after the European Central Bank broke all the rules and started to buy government bonds and provide unlimited liquidity. Yet the euro remains at very weak levels (having fallen as much as 20 percent between January 2010 and

June 2010) while credit spreads for countries such as Portugal, Ireland, Spain, and Greece hit record levels. At the time of publication, it is still unclear how the sovereign debt crisis will play out and the magnitude of its impact.

Even if the markets stabilize, individual countries have pledged to aggressively reduce their budget deficits, which means spending cuts and tax increases that should curtail Eurozone growth as the belt buckles in Europe get tighter and tighter. It is too early to count the losers against the winners on this, but those who anticipated the move would have come out on top once again. Some funds have bought credit default swaps on Spanish, Italian, and Irish debt as a sort of insurance in the case of default. Just think— investors who shorted euros when Greece's troubles began in late 2009 could have made as much as 20 percent by the end of June 2010.

The subprime and the sovereign debt crisis showed us how we cannot focus solely on what is happening in our own little part of the world because, as we have seen, the problems in one country like the United States could destroy the economies of other countries. As the world's largest trading partner, it is easy to understand why everyone else would be affected by the troubles in the United States, but in recent years, problems in other countries also had a ripple effect on other parts of the world.

Countries as far away as Australia have complained about the impact of the European debt crisis on their local economy. Even big and mighty China has found Europe and Greece's problem nerve-racking, illustrating just how interconnected the world really is.

The Rise of Currencies

The two most recent crises have focused attention on the foreign exchange market. In many ways, currencies are one of the best confidence indicators for a country. When foreign investors are optimistic about the outlook for a country, they tend to buy the currency and use those funds to invest in domestic stocks or bonds. However, when they grow concerned for economic, political, or social reasons, they will sell their foreign holdings, dump the currency, and move the money home. When this happens on a large scale, it can cause a major move in the currency and force the government to address the situation.

If a currency becomes too weak, as the euro did during the sovereign debt crisis, there are concerns about inflationary pressures. If it becomes too strong, exporters cry for help because it reduces the competiveness of their goods. Extreme moves in currencies can also affect the earnings of multinational companies. For example, if a company has a lot of accounts payable in other currencies, a strong local currency will reduce the value of the accounts payable while a weak local currency will increase it. At the same time, exporters typically love a weak currency and despise a strong one.

Currencies matter in different ways to different people; we will discuss this in further detail in Chapter 2. The subprime crisis that began in the United States and the European sovereign debt crisis may have lifted currencies from the business news to the headline news, but the popularity of currencies is not particularly new. Over the past 10 years, the forex market has grown significantly. Back in 2004, the Bank for International Settlements reported that the daily turnover in the forex market was approximately $1.9 trillion. When they released their triennial survey again in 2010, volume had increased to $4 trillion. For the first time ever, banks also did more transactions with "other financial institutions" (think retail forex brokers) than with other banks. Therefore, a large part of the growth in foreign exchange can be attributed to individual investors discovering the opportunities in forex trading.

Turning Headlines into Opportunities

If history tells us anything (and we know it does), there will be more crises, large and small, in various parts of the world over the next 10 years. When they occur, you will have the choice of being on the offense or the defense. So as my Aunt Judy always asked, how will you turn lemons into lemonade? Hindsight is always 20/20; in retrospect, it is easy say that dot-com companies with zero to negative earnings did not deserve their sky-high valuations or that people would eventually stop paying astronomical prices for homes, especially as inventory flooded the market and consumers became overburdened with debt. The key is to not get caught up in the madness and be able to think rationally about whether the price of the asset is appropriate given the risks and valuations.

Of course, this is easier said than done, but not impossible if we consider the different ways that a small investor could have capitalized on the recent crises.

Let's start off with the subprime crisis. As we all know, the crisis caused a number of financial institutions to fail. Some were seized by the government; others were rescued, sold to competitors, or forced into bankruptcy. Although some people may argue that it is immoral to profit from someone else's misfortune, that was how Soros, Paulson, and Templeton made a large part of their wealth. Exhibit 1.1 is a daily chart illustrating how the U.S. dollar and the Japanese yen—known as the USD/JPY currency pair—behaved after the failure of major financial institutions. The first arrow points to the time

Exhibit 1.1 The Reaction of the U.S. Dollar and Japanese Yen to the Failure of Major Financial Institutions

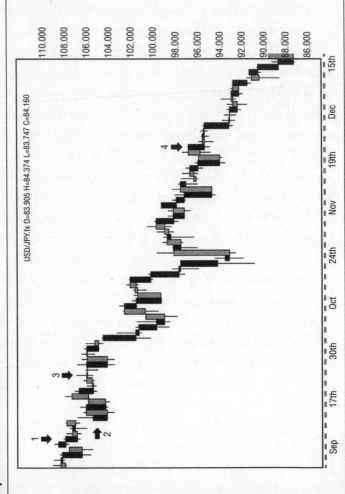

Source: GFT Dealbook 360.

when Fannie Mae and Freddie Mac were seized. The second arrow indicates when Lehman Brothers filed for bankruptcy. The third arrow points to when Washington Mutual collapsed, and the fourth indicates when the U.S. government was forced to rescue Citigroup. As you can see, in each case the currency pair extended its losses. Even rescues or acquisitions failed to lift the dollar on the fear that more trouble would come. Those investors who sold dollars against the Japanese yen during the subprime crisis were handsomely rewarded.

Moving on to the European sovereign debt crisis, as the events in Greece unfolded and it became more apparent that the country was headed for financial trouble, credit rating agencies began to slash its debt rating. A credit rating agency is a company that assigns credit ratings that are meant to show the likelihood of an issuer defaulting on its debt. Ratings are given in the form of letter grades, almost like a report card. When a country's rating is downgraded, it means that, for one reason or another, they've become more likely to default on their debt. In October 2009, one of the leading credit rating agencies, Fitch Ratings, downgraded Greece's sovereign debt rating to A–, triggering what later turned into a 20 percent sell-off in the euro (EUR) against the U.S. dollar. As in the case of the USD/JPY, each time Greece or another sick country within the Eurozone was downgraded, the EUR/USD sold off. These downgrades set off waves of concern among investors because it meant that the country was moving closer and closer to defaulting on its loans. By April 2010, Greece's debt ratings had been slashed to junk levels. One way to capitalize on the crisis would have been to turn the headlines into trading opportunities—or, in other words, sell when the panic begins because one downgrade will often be followed by another.

Even if you don't feel comfortable turning the stories into opportunities and prefer to trade on chart levels, you could have capitalized on the moves in both currency pairs by selling the breaks of key levels. For example, 105, 100, and 95 were all important psychological levels in the USD/JPY. The same is true for 1.45, 1.40, 1.35, and 1.30 in the EUR/USD.

Currencies are trending in nature, especially during times of panic, and therefore, joining a move may yield better results than fading it. If you are not patient enough to sit with a trade for long, you can consider something shorter term in the direction of the prevailing market sentiment. For example, after a downgrade, you may want to look for opportunities to sell the EUR/USD for a short-term potential profit, assuming that trouble begets more trouble with a stop to limit the losses.

Get It? Got It? Good!

- Financial crises are becoming increasingly common.
- But not everyone is a loser! Legendary investors like Sir John Templeton have shown that there are bargains to be found during times of crisis.
- Some professional money managers such as George Soros and John Paulson were smart to anticipate recent market meltdowns and profited big-time.
- In times of crisis, currency trading is a way to turn headlines into opportunities.

Chapter Two

Rubles and Bahts and Euros—Oh, My!

Forex Isn't as Foreign as You Think

THE WORLD SHOWCASE IN DISNEY WORLD'S EPCOT Center is a series of intricately built pavilions that represent 11 countries, giving visitors a taste of different cultures and culinary specialties. It was built in 1982, 17 years before the euro, the official currency of the Eurozone, was even introduced, and yet it manages to capture the heart and spirit of the euro.

In the World Showcase, you can walk from one pavilion or "country" to another without a passport, which makes it easier to visit and shop in more than one "country" during a single trip. Furthermore, the same currency can be used to buy something in Japan or Italy without having to worry about exchange rates. In the same manner, the euro provides these benefits for its members by making it easier for companies and consumers in different countries to do business with each other by eliminating exchange rate conversions and unnecessary paperwork. As a result, intra-region trade has increased significantly. If you have been to the World Showcase, then you can understand why the euro or a single currency is so important. Imagine how cumbersome it would be to exchange currencies and carry a passport every time you traveled from New York to California or Florida.

Even if you have never been to the World Showcase, the forex market may not be as foreign as you think, particularly if you have ever traveled abroad. It is no secret that the worst place to exchange your money is at the airport. Most travelers who exchange their money at the airport are desperate for some local currency for a taxi to their hotels. Savvier travelers will either use credit cards because the exchange rate is slightly more favorable or take cash out of the ATM. However, even then, foreign exchange fees may be added to the transactions.

Being a seasoned traveler, I know that the smartest thing to do is to exchange your money at foreign exchange shops downtown where competition is usually heavier and the exchange rates are better.

On a recent business trip to Australia, I compared different exchange rates. At the time, the market rate for the Australian dollar and the U.S. dollar was 0.8750 and of course I did not expect to get that from anyone. At the airport in Sydney, they were offering currency conversion from U.S. dollars to Australian dollars at a rate of 93 cents per dollar. In the central business district, there were vendors offering exchange rates of 89 cents while my American Express card charged me a rate of 0.9045 with a few bucks tacked on for fees.

In today's global markets, keeping on top of the movements in exchange rates has become extremely important. In this chapter, we will explore how currency fluctuations affect companies, investors, property owners, and anyone who does business overseas.

Waking Up the "Local" Investor

If you are an American who invests exclusively in the U.S. stock market and could care less about exchange rates, it may be time to wake up. Following exchange rate movements can help you make better investment decisions. During the month following the end of each business quarter, everyone from bank analysts to longer term investors are scouring data on existing and new product lines for any information on the quarter's potential sales and profits. Most likely, unless they have inside information, everyone in the market is looking at the same news releases. However, there is one consideration that rarely pops into the mind of the American investor but can mean the difference between a good quarter and a bad one—the impact of currency fluctuations on a company's bottom line. Too many times, companies that are expected to report good earnings for the quarter disappoint due to either a currency's depreciation or appreciation during those three months, as good sales are offset by adverse conversion rates.

Currencies affect different types of U.S. companies in different ways. McDonalds, Burger King, and Starbucks, for example, have franchise businesses where they license the right to operate their stores to local partners abroad in return for a part of their revenue. Since this revenue is earned in foreign currencies, it has to be converted back to U.S. dollars. Therefore, a strong U.S. dollar tends to hurt their profitability while a weak U.S. dollar promotes it. Imagine that McDonalds sells Big Macs in the U.K. for 2 British pounds each at an exchange rate of 1.80. For U.S.-based McDonalds, who doesn't change its international prices often and franchises some but not all of its U.K. operations, that would mean revenue of $3.60 per Big Mac. Now suppose that the British pound weakens 20 percent, bringing the exchange rate down to 1.44. The 2 British pounds that McDonalds charges for each Big Mac now equals revenue of only $2.88 instead of $3.60.

On a per Big Mac basis the difference is small, but compounded by the millions of Big Macs sold abroad, you can see how a strong dollar can hurt companies such as McDonald's, which earned 40 percent of its revenue from Europe in 2009. In the first quarter of 2010, McDonalds competitor Burger King said they expect foreign exchange to shave earnings by up to two pennies per share. Exhibit 2.1 illustrates how a 20 percent rise and fall in the value of the British pound and U.S. dollar exchange rate can affect the amount of money McDonald's makes per Big Mac.

Similarly, technology firms with a big dependence on international sales such as Google, Priceline, and Expedia

Exhibit 2.1 The GBP/USD Exchange Rate Impacts McDonalds Revenues

Price of Big Mac in Pounds	Exchange Rate	Revenue in U.S. Dollars
2£	Rises to 2.16	$4.32
2£	1.80	$3.60
2£	Falls to 1.44	$2.88

suffer when the U.S. dollar is strong because it reduces the value of their foreign earnings. In general, when the dollar becomes too strong, U.S. multinational companies are faced with the tough dilemma of raising prices to keep margins intact or holding prices and taking a cut in profitability. With a strong dollar, we tend to see more disappointments than surprises in U.S. earnings, but with a weak dollar, there tends to be more positive than negative surprises (i.e., each Big Mac sold abroad translates into more U.S. dollars).

Companies with extensive imports or exports are also impacted by currency fluctuations. In general, U.S. companies that have significant accounts payable in foreign currencies (such as importers) usually benefit from dollar strength and are hurt by dollar weakness. The companies that have a significant amount of accounts receivable denominated in foreign currencies (such as U.S. exporters) usually benefit from dollar weakness and suffer when the dollar is strong. The industries with the greatest foreign sales exposure are energy, technology, and consumer staples. Companies that produce and export commodities also benefit from a weaker dollar because it drives commodity prices higher. There are countless other examples of how currencies can affect earnings and savvy equity investors could find an edge by monitoring currency movements during the quarter in addition to sales reports. The same theory applies even if your domestic market is not the United States.

Dabbling in Foreign Markets

For people who are savvy enough to invest in foreign markets, exchange rate movements are even more important because movements in exchange rates can either compound returns or diminish them.

Imagine you were an American investor looking to invest in Asia back in 2009 because you believed Asia would be fairly immune to the financial crisis. You decided to invest in the Singapore market because Singapore is considered the Switzerland of Asia, everyone speaks English, the government is stable, and it is a well-developed economy. You bought shares of Singapore Airlines (SIA) because you believed that travel to Asia would increase due to the country's tourism initiative and because the airline has a fantastic reputation for its service and quality. In January 2009, you bought 100 shares of SIA at S$10.50 per share for a total cost of 10,500 Singapore dollars. At the time, the U.S. dollar/Singapore dollar exchange rate was approximately 1.46, which meant that the cost in U.S. dollars was $7,191. In December 2009, you cashed in on your investment and returned your funds home. By then, SIA shares were worth approximately S$14.75, which put the value of your total investment at

S$14,750. In one year, you would have made a whopping 40.47 percent! When you converted the Singapore dollars back into U.S. dollars, the bank gave you $10,461. A 40.47 percent return on $7,191 should have given you approximately US$10,102, not US$10,461. It seems like a bank error, but it wasn't. Between January and December of that year, the Singapore dollar strengthened against the U.S. dollar, earning you another 5 percent because of exchange rate fluctuations!

But exchange rates can rise just as easily as they can fall. In the first six months of 2010, the euro fell 14.5 percent against the U.S. dollar. If an American invested in the German stock market at the beginning of the year, their return in the equity market would have been negative 2.56 percent, but actual losses in U.S. dollar terms would have been closer to 17 percent due to exchange rate fluctuations.

Investors with offshore bank accounts or money abroad also need to know about exchange rates. We have all watched movies about international spies who have money in bank accounts around the world. Most of our lives are not that glamorous but maybe you know someone with a bank account offshore, or in another country. My good friend Marcia moved to London for work last year and opened a bank account in the U.K. She kept her account back home because her work contract is only for three

years, but for now she is paid in British pounds and her
paychecks are deposited into her London bank account.
Her salary is GBP 50,000 a year.

Recently, I received a frantic call from Marcia, who
was desperate for some advice. Her career doesn't require
that she follow exchange rates, but she had overheard
coworkers in the U.K. complaining about the cost of
traveling to the United States. Marcia wondered why, so
she asked a few questions and found out that the British
pound had fallen 7.5 percent against the U.S. dollar,
which meant that she received an implicit 7.5 percent pay
cut because of exchange rates, or the equivalent of roughly
US$5,000 (at an exchange rate of US$1.50 per British
pound). Although she was worried about the recent drop,
she was even more concerned about the possibility of further depreciation in the pound, which would have made
her wages worth less in U.S. dollar terms. One of the
things that Marcia could have done was use option contracts to protect against a move lower in the pound or to
convert her money back into U.S. dollars on a more regular basis. For other people who may have made perma-
nent moves to another country because of immigration or
other factors and kept a bank account in their home country, the same logic applies. If there is a big currency move,
the value of your savings in the foreign bank account will
be affected.

It has also become more common for investors to dabble in real estate in different countries. For example, the Chinese are flush with cash these days. It has become so popular for the Chinese to take trips to the United States, Canada, or Australia to visit property that there is a new term known as "real estate tourism." Outside of the United States, foreign property investment is extremely popular. I attended a property expo in Australia once where Americans were selling land and homes in Florida at discounted rates.

When a currency is weak, there tends to be more property investment by foreigners; when it is strong, foreign investors will shy away because of the increased premium created by the higher exchange rate. At the same time there are also Americans who have property abroad— for example, you may be collecting rent on an apartment that you own in Paris near the Arc de Triomphe and the tenant wires you money in euros that are then converted into U.S. dollars by your bank. In that case, if the U.S. dollar strengthens, you would likely receive fewer dollars when the euros are converted, but if it weakens, then you would probably receive more U.S. dollars.

Small-Business Owners and Financial Officers

Foreign exchange risk also affects anyone who conducts international business or trading activity, including small businesses and financial officers of medium- to large-sized companies. Buying or selling goods or services denominated in foreign currencies can immediately expose a company to foreign exchange risk.

For example, one of my nephew's favorite stores is Kid Robot in New York City. Unlike regular toy stores, this store sells quirky toys imported directly from Japan. If the store does not use a distributor, then it most likely has to grapple with the regular fluctuations in the Japanese yen. If the yen rises in value, the toys that they import to New York become more expensive. This may also be true for your local video rental store that carries a large selection of foreign films. If the films are imported directly from the respective country, then its price could be affected by exchange rates.

Small businesses usually write off the movements in currencies as a cost of doing business, but large companies may choose to hedge their exposures because they are importing hundreds of thousands of dollars worth of products. The payment may be due immediately or a few months later depending upon the terms. If the payments are delayed, it is even more important to hedge foreign risk. Take the example of a U.S. company that purchased AU$100,000 worth of products from an Australian company to be paid six months later. At that time, the chief financial officer allocated US$80,000 for the payment (which was the value of the contract when it was drawn up), but six months later finds that US$85,000 converts to only $88,888 Australian dollars, which means the company needs to scramble to find another AU$11,112 to pay the bill.

What about a U.S. company that sells all American widgets abroad? How will they be affected by exchange rates? Let's assume a small-business owner sells an average of 10,000 widgets per year at a price of 20 euros per widget. At the beginning of the year, the EUR/USD exchange rate is 1.30 and so you, the business owner, anticipated revenue to be US$26,000. Exhibit 2.2 shows how revenues would be affected by a 10 cent change in the exchange rate. If the exchange rate fell by 10 cents, revenue would be $20,000 less than expected, but if it rises by 10 cents, it would $20,000 more. Since exchange rates can rise just as easily as they can fall, it's absolutely essential for companies that import and export any

Exhibit 2.2   How Changes in the EUR/USD Exchange Rate Affects Revenues

Number of Widgets	Price per Widget in Euros	Revenue in Euros	Exchange Rate	Revenue in U.S. Dollars
10,000	20	200,000	1.20	$240,000
10,000	20	200,000	1.30	$260,000
10,000	20	200,000	1.40	$280,000

sizeable amount of products to monitor the foreign exchange markets and manage the risk.

As the number of foreign exchange products increases, so do the ways to hedge foreign exchange risk. The most common way for a company to hedge away the risk is through the use of derivative contracts such as forwards, futures, or options. A forward contract is an agreement to exchange a specific amount of currency at a specific rate on a specific date. A futures contract acts in the same way except that futures contracts are standardized and rarely customized. An option, on the other hand, can be standardized (traded on an exchange) or purchased over the counter and customized to the exact business requirements. Options give the buyer the right but not the obligation to buy or sell the currency at a specified rate. If the rate is not advantageous, the buyer can abandon the transaction. Futures and options are not suitable for everyone. Carefully consider whether trading is appropriate for you in light of your experience, objectives, financial resources, and other relevant circumstances.

Some companies may also opt for a money market hedge that can be similar to an immediate forex conversion if the company has the money available. If they do not, they can borrow in their local money market and use those funds to buy a money market security in the foreign currency with the same maturity (borrowing costs and money market rate will apply) and settle both at the end of the period.

What's Your Agenda?

Different people participate in the forex market for different reasons. One of the most common questions that new forex traders ask is whether forex trading is a zero sum game, meaning that whenever one trader makes money, another loses. To answer that question, consider whether or not you think a traveler exchanging currencies in a foreign country or a company hedging foreign exchange risk would consider the exchange to be a loss? Probably not. When I go to Australia, I exchange my U.S. dollars into Australian dollars and then forget about it. After exchanging their currencies, most travelers hurry off to enjoy the views from the Eiffel Tower or sit on a beach in Thailand. As for a medium-sized company importing widgets, the goal of hedging foreign exchange risk is to stop worrying about it because, once a transaction is hedged, the focus should be on selling the goods and moving the inventory.

Currency movements affect the financial decisions of equity investors, small-business owners, expats, and even travelers in more ways than anyone can imagine. Yet many companies do not fully hedge their forex risk because they want to take advantage of currency movements in their favor. So wouldn't it be great to be able to figure out where currencies could be headed and whether a trend will last or fade? Next, we'll be talking about strategies and tools that can help do just that, and I can't wait to share them.

Get It? Got It? Good!

- Currencies are not as foreign as you think! They are a part of everyone's lives already.
- Even casual travelers can learn a lot about currency trading by considering the exchange rates and fees they pay in different countries.
- Companies that have franchises abroad are affected by every move in the currency markets. If you're an investor in one of those companies, pay attention.
- If you invest in foreign companies or real estate, currency fluctuations can increase or decrease returns.
- Small-business owners and other companies that import products from abroad should know the importance of hedging against foreign exchange risk!

Chapter Three

The A to Zs of Forex

~

Basic Knowledge You Need to Have

BUT BEFORE GETTING TOO EXCITED ABOUT HOW currency trading works, it is important to get the basics down first; to do that, let's grab our backpacks and head back to school to learn the A to Zs of forex trading.

Alpha.   Most businesses dabble in the forex market to reduce their exposure to big exchange rate fluctuations, but some companies also want to earn alpha. Alpha is the "excess" return that a manager earns above and beyond a benchmark index like the S&P 500 or a risk-free investment such as Treasuries. Alpha is how fund managers earn their keep because there is no point in investing with the fund and paying a management or performance fee if all that they can do is earn the same return or less than that of the S&P 500. Investors and traders turn to the forex market because of the desire to earn additional alpha.

Base Currency and Counter Currency.   It takes two to tango; the value of a currency is always based upon another currency. For example, if the euro/U.S. dollar exchange rate is 1.50, it means that one euro can be exchanged for 1.50 U.S. dollars. If the U.S. dollar/Japanese yen exchange rate is 110, then one U.S. dollar can be exchanged for 110 Japanese yen. The first currency that is quoted in a currency pair is known as the base currency and the second is known as the counter currency. The symbols can be interchanged, but there are industry standards. When the euro was first launched in 1999, the European Central Bank actually stipulated that the euro must be a base currency. The currencies of other countries that are currently or were previously under the Crown, such as the British pound and Australian and New Zealand dollars, are typically base currencies as well, while the Japanese yen, Swiss franc, and Canadian dollar are almost always counter currencies. The U.S. dollar can be either a base or counter currency, depending upon what currency it is quoted against.

Currencies. As of 2010, there are approximately 150 currencies in the world, but not all of them are actively traded because some are available for trading and others aren't, depending upon whether they are a fixed or floating currency and if the government permits it. The most commonly used currency in the world is the U.S. dollar. In fact, more than 85 percent of all currency transactions involve the U.S. dollar. How often a currency is used is extremely important for investors and speculators because it reflects how easy or hard it is to get out of a position in that currency. Therefore, I always say that if you are investing or trading for alpha, it is best to stick with the most actively traded currencies, which are the U.S. dollar, euro, Japanese yen, British pound, Swiss franc, Australian dollar, and Canadian dollar. Exhibit 3.1

Exhibit 3.1   Codes, Symbols, and Market Share for Key Currencies

Currency	Code	Symbol	% Daily Share
U.S. dollar	USD	$	84.9%
Euro	EUR	€	39.1%
Japanese yen	JPY	¥	19.0%
British pound	GBP	£	12.9%
Australian dollar	AUD	$	7.6%
Swiss franc	CHF	Fr	6.4%
Canadian dollar	CAD	$	5.3%

Source: BIS 2007 Triennial Survey.

lists each currency, code, symbol, and the share that each of these currencies has of the daily turnover in the currency market according to the Bank of International Settlements' Triennial FX Survey (2010).

Dealers.   Corporations, investors, and speculators access the foreign exchange market through dealers, who can be the direct counterparty or a middleman. For most travelers, the airport kiosk is their foreign exchange dealer. Corporations, mutual funds, and hedge fund managers, on the other hand, directly call in to the dealing or sales trading desks of Goldman Sachs or Citigroup to conduct their transactions. Individuals are usually not trading large enough amounts to matter to a big bank like Goldman Sachs and so, instead, they will usually access the market through a retail forex broker or an exchange.

Exchange.   One of the unique aspects of the forex market is that there is no formalized exchange such as the NYSE (New York Stock Exchange) or the CME (Chicago Mercantile Exchange). Underlying currency transactions are done over the counter, which means they are handled directly by dealers. The lack of a formal exchange is probably the main reason some people are hesitant about dabbling in currencies, but the competition in the market has made pricing extremely competitive and forced many forex dealers to offer free educational resources and tools that would normally cost hundreds of dollars a month.

The governments of many countries have also instituted tough rules and capitalization requirements for the dealers to protect investors and traders.

Fundamentals. Generally speaking, the movements in currencies reflect how investors and speculators feel about the economic outlook of one country relative to another. Looking at concrete economic data or hard numbers to compare the outlook of two countries is known as fundamental analysis. There are many different ways to analyze the markets on a fundamental basis; the topic is so important that an entire chapter is dedicated to it.

Going Long and Short. One of the interesting things about currencies is that in a forex transaction, you are going long one currency and short another simultaneously. This is important because it means that you are exposed to the fluctuations of two currencies. For example, the Australian dollar/New Zealand dollar exchange rate will rise if investors buy Australian dollars, sell New Zealand dollars (NZD), or both. Theoretically, if the AUD and NZD rise at the exact same time by the same amount, the exchange rate will not move—just like with the tango, nothing happens except toes being stepped on when both dancers move forward.

Hedging. Most companies dabble in the forex market to hedge or offset the currency-related exposure of their import or export activities, but they are not the only ones that can benefit from hedging. When stock markets around the world collapsed during the global financial crisis, investors poured into the safety of the U.S. dollar and low-yielding currencies. As a result, investors who wanted to protect against additional losses in stocks could have hedged their positions by buying U.S. dollars, Swiss francs, and Japanese yen. Hedging accounts for a lot of the big transactions that flow through the forex market.

Interest Rates.   If I had to pick only one thing to determine where currencies are headed, it would certainly be interest rates. Currencies are basically little interest-bearing commodities, and almost every country has an official interest rate that determines the borrowing cost of the government, its banks, and citizens—this is the rate that sets your credit card and mortgage payments. The interest rate is usually manipulated by the central bank to control growth and inflation in their local economy, but it can also increase or decrease the attractiveness of a currency. In this modern day and age, it is extremely easy for investors to shift their money from one country to another in search of the highest yield. For most of 2010, Americans could not find a bank in the United States that would offer them a savings account with an annual interest rate of more than 2 percent. During that same year, anyone shopping for a savings account in Australia could easily find a bank offering an interest rate greater than 5 percent. Therefore, if you could, would you prefer to have your money in an Australian or U.S. bank account? This thinking is exactly what caused the Australian dollar to outperform the U.S. dollar in the first half of 2010. However, it's a bit more complicated than that—investors move their money from one country to another not just based upon where interest rates are at but where they are headed. So it is very possible for a country with a lower interest rate to attract more money than a country with a higher interest rate.

J-Curve.   Think about how the letter J is written. First, when your pen hits the page, your hand draws a slight slanted line downward. The line quickly turns into a curve that rolls into a smile and extends into a large tail upward. Writing the letter J reminds us of recovery followed by strength, and this is how many experts believe that a country's trade deficit will respond to a fall in the currency. Currency movements have a big impact on trade activity. According to the theory of many economists, after a currency experiences a very large decline, the country's trade deficit will worsen initially before it improves. On the most basic level, currencies move because of trade-related supply and demand. When a clothing retailer in New York needs to import handmade

Italian suits to be sold at a boutique on Madison Avenue in New York City, at some point or another, the retailer needs to sell U.S. dollars and buy euros to pay for the order. If the euro were to fall significantly, the Italian suit manufacturer would receive more orders for suits from Americans, but not immediately because it takes some time for American retailers to realize that the exchange rate has fallen, sell existing inventory, browse the catalogues, discuss designs, and negotiate prices before they can place a new order. However, companies in Europe that import from other countries will feel the pain from the drop in the exchange rate almost immediately because they will not be able to adjust the amount that they import until their existing orders and payments are fulfilled. A weak currency will eventually help a country's trade activities, but not before it does some damage.

Kiwi. The kiwi is the nickname for New Zealand's currency because the flightless birds, a national symbol, are native to the country. The U.S. dollar is oftentimes called the buck or greenback, the British pound may be referred to as sterling, cable, or just the pound. The Canadian dollar is known as the loonie (the loon is a popular aquatic bird found throughout Canada), while the Australian dollar is referred to as the Aussie. Become familiar with these nicknames because they are used interchangeably with the official names of the currencies.

Leverage.   Understanding leverage and controlling it divides the winners from the losers in the forex market. Leverage is almost always described as a double-edged sword, and rightfully so. It is what attracts most speculators to the forex market but also what turns them away. To leverage means to lean on something to gain an advantage. In trading, you leverage by using borrowed money to magnify your investment. Most forex brokers will offer their clients 50 times leverage on the major currencies, which means that with $2,000, a trader can control up to $100,000 worth of a currency. Sounds great right? If the value of your investment increases by 2 percent, you would have made $2,000 (2 percent of $100,000) for a return of 100 percent on your initial investment. But not so fast—the currency can move against you just as easily as it can move in your favor, so the 100 percent gain can also turn into a 100 percent loss. Therefore, leverage needs to be controlled. Just because the broker is offering you that much leverage, it doesn't mean that you need to exhaust it. If you bought an entire box of chocolate chip cookies, should you eat them all in one sitting? Not unless you want your waistline to expand. Professional traders who survive in the forex market will usually not risk more than 5 percent of their account on any one trade, and using stops can be a good way to limit the downside risk of leverage.

Margin. Margin is another way of looking at leverage. In the previous example, $2,000 would control $100,000 worth of currency, which meant that a 2 percent margin deposit was required for the ability to use 50 to 1 leverage. The margin is not the maximum amount that you can lose on your position because your maximum loss is based upon the actual size of your position. It is how much the broker requires you to allocate in your account for each open position. In the event of a margin call, when your account falls below the margin requirement to keep the positions active, your broker will close some or all open positions.

No Uptick Rule. Back when the markets crashed in October 2008, it was very difficult for speculators to short into a rapidly falling market (countries like the United States require an uptick before a stock can be shorted). One possible way to participate in the sell-off at the time would have been to buy U.S. dollars and Japanese yen because there is no uptick rule in the forex market; in times of overwhelming nervousness, low-yielding currencies are in big demand. Investors who wanted to offset their losses in stocks could have bought dollars and yen.

Order Types. There are many different ways to enter and exit your forex positions; if you already trade equities, the order types should be familiar. The standard orders that most brokers offer are limit entry orders, market entry orders, fixed stop, trailing stop, and market exit orders. The orders can be good till cancelled (GTC), good for the day (GTD), or one cancels other (OCO).

Pip.   If you have ever talked to a forex trader, you may have heard them say that the EUR/USD has moved 150 pips and wondered what the word *pip* meant. A pip is basically fancy forex lingo for the word *point* and stands for percentage in point, which is the smallest standardized incremental price change for a currency. Most currency pairs, such as the EUR/USD, are quoted out to four decimal points, which means that if the EUR/USD has moved from 1.5015 to 1.5016, it has moved one pip. Currency pairs that involve the Japanese yen have only two numbers after the decimal, so a one-pip move in those pairs would be .01. Since a pip is worth a different dollar amount for each currency, it is very important to know how

How to Calculate Pip Values

Example #1 USD/JPY

For a currency pair that has the U.S. dollar as a base currency (quoted first in the pair), simply divide the smallest price change by the current quote and multiply it by the amount of currency traded. If we trade 100,000 units of USD/JPY at a current exchange rate of 89.00, the pip value would be calculated in the following steps:

(Continues)

HOW TO CALCULATE
PIP VALUES (*Continued*)

1. .01 (pip amount) divided by 89.00 (USD/JPY exchange rate) = .00011235 (pip value per dollar)

2. .00011235 (pip value per dollar) × 100,000 (amount of dollars traded) = $11.23

Example #2 EUR/USD

For a currency pair where the U.S. dollar is the counter currency (quoted second in the pair), there is one additional step. Follow the same method as the above and then convert the amount back into U.S. dollars by multiplying the pip cost by the exchange rate. If we trade 100,000 units of EUR/USD at a current exchange rate of 1.2250, the pip value would be calculated in the following steps:

1. .0001 (pip amount) divided by 1.2250 (EUR/USD exchange rate) = 0.000081632 (pip value per euro)

2. 0.000081632 × 100,000 (amount of dollars traded) = 8.16 (pip value in euros)

3. Convert pip value in euros into dollars. 8.16 × 1.2250 (EUR/USD exchange rate) = $10 (pip value in U.S. dollars)

Many free pip calculators can be found on the Internet and some brokers will list the fluctuating pip values on their dealing stations.

to calculate pip values; otherwise, you won't know how much a move in a currency is worth in your account.

Quotes. Since there is no formalized exchange in the forex market, brokers may have different buy and sell prices (known as quotes) at any point in time. The buy price is also known as the ask price and the sell price is called the bid. When shopping for a forex broker, it is important to compare their quotes to see who gives you the best pricing.

Rollover.   Rollover is unique to the forex market because each currency has an interest rate that is determined by the central bank of the country. By going long and short two currencies at the same time, forex traders are eligible to earn interest on the currency that they have bought and are required to pay interest on the currency that they have sold. For example, in 2010, Australia offered a much higher interest rate than the United States. Anyone going long Australian dollars against U.S. dollars would be eligible to earn interest on positions held overnight, whereas anyone who shorted the AUD/USD would be obligated to pay interest. The daily interest amount is calculated by subtracting the annual U.S. interest rate from the Australian rate and dividing it by the number of days in a year.

Spot.   Like the word *pip*, the word *spot* is another forex-specific term that is used often by investors and traders. The spot price references the current market price; a spot trade is simply a transaction in the currency or commodity. Because currencies and commodities are traded often in the futures and options markets, *spot* can also mean the underlying or physical item that is being transacted.

Technical Analysis. Some forex investors will attempt to predict the direction where currencies are headed using fundamental analysis (FA), while others like to use technical analysis (TA), the art of chart reading. Many new traders actually prefer technicals over fundamentals because the same strategies and techniques that are used in stock trading can be used in currency trading. The forex market trades 24 hours a day, which means that the points in the charts are created using more samples, increasing its statistical significance. If you are unfamiliar with forex but very skilled at technical analysis, the best thing to do would be to use what you know, especially because this style of analysis is already a very popular trading and investment style among forex traders.

Units of Trade. Although currencies can be traded in any amounts, there are standardized units of trade. A standard lot in a currency pair is 100,000 units of trade. A mini lot is 1/10th the size of a standard lot and refers to 10,000 units of trade; micro lots are 1/100th the size of a standard lot or 1,000 units of currency. Unless someone is trading a very significant amount of money, micro lots give most traders more flexibility because the smaller lot sizes allows them to ease in and out of positions. Micro lots are useful for new traders who want to add in the psychological element of trading real money but are not comfortable enough to commit a more significant amount of capital.

Volatility.   Forex brokers offer trading in as many as 120 different currency pairs; this extensive range of options can be compelling but only if you understand that currencies can vary significantly in volatility. For example, Exhibit 3.2 shows that the average daily trading range for EUR/CHF over the past 10 years was 66 pips, while the average range in GBP/JPY was 256 pips. This means that on an intraday basis, GBP/JPY is going to be far more volatile than EUR/CHF. Therefore, a 40-pip stop may be very significant for EUR/CHF but very insignificant for GBP/JPY. Forex traders like to consider GBP/JPY the "Google" of the forex market, because it is an exceptionally volatile currency pair with wide intraday swings.

Whipsaw.   Economic data and big events can create a lot of whipsaw in currencies; therefore, it is essential to know what can potentially move the markets. Thankfully, the same things that are important to the stock market are important to the forex market. For example, central bank rate decisions and labor markets reports such as non-farm payrolls are very big market movers, while the pieces of data that are rarely discussed in the media such as the ABC consumer confidence index usually have very little impact on currencies.

Xenocurrency.   The term *Xenocurrency* is not used often, but it is important. A Xenocurrency refers to a currency that is traded outside its borders; a good example

Exhibit 3.2   Daily Trading Ranges for Key Currencies

Currency Pair	Daily Range
EUR/CHF	66
EUR/GBP	89
NZD/CAD	95
NZD/CHF	100
AUD/CAD	103
AUD/CHF	110
CAD/CHF	111
USD/JPY	112
NZD/USD	115
USD/CHF	120
CHF/JPY	128
AUD/USD	130
NZD/JPY	132
USD/CAD	141
CAD/JPY	150
EUR/USD	152
AUD/JPY	156
EUR/CAD	163
GBP/CHF	191
EUR/AUD	193
GBP/USD	196
EUR/JPY	196
GBP/CAD	219
GBP/AUD	254
GBP/JPY	256
EUR/NZD	279

is the Chinese yuan. The yuan is not actively traded in China but it is traded as a non-deliverable forward (NDF), which is a cash-settled contract that allows speculators to take a view on where the yuan may be headed in one week's or one year's time. Mainland companies are not allowed to participate in the NDF market because it is conducted offshore.

Yield. Currencies are oftentimes referred to as either high yield or low yield. High-yield currencies offer more attractive interest rates compared to low-yield currencies. When investors are optimistic, they generally like to buy high-yielding currencies and fund those purchases by selling low-yielding ones, creating what is called a carry trade. When they grow nervous, they will unwind those trades by selling the high-yielding currencies and buying back the low-yielding ones. This is one of the main reasons the currency market will oftentimes move in lockstep with equities because equities rally when investors are optimistic and sell off when they are pessimistic.

Zones. The last important item to know about the forex market is that it is open for trading 24 hours a day, 5.5 days a week. Trading begins on Sunday evening when the Sydney and Tokyo markets open and continues around the clock until Friday afternoon when the U.S. market closes. Being open 24 hours a day means that traders can access the market at their leisure. For example, if you

Exhibit 3.3   Unofficial Open and Closes

Time Zone	Open (GMT)	Close (GMT)
Tokyo	0:00	8:00
London	7:00	17:00
New York	12:00	21:00

work during the day, you can trade at night or wake up a few hours early and trade in the morning with basically the same liquidity as during the day. The forex market is broken up into three different time zones—Tokyo, London, and New York. Exhibit 3.3 lists the opening and closing hours of each market. Approximately 70 percent of the total average range that a currency pair fluctuates in usually occurs during the European trading hours; 80 percent of the total average range of trading usually occurs during U.S. trading hours. Just these percentages alone tell day traders that if they cannot sit at the screen all day, the best time to trade is the U.S. and European overlap between 12:00 and 17:00 GMT. The next best time zone to trade is during the Tokyo and European session overlap when both Asian and European traders have the opportunity to respond to European economic data. The London open can also be particularly volatile as European traders react to overnight developments.

And those, my friends, are the A to Zs of forex trading!

Chapter Four

Step Right Up

~

Getting Started in Forex

THE WAY KIDS APPROACH AN AMUSEMENT PARK is very similar to the way some adults approach trading. All they want to do is get their tickets, run in, and explore. They have no plan or strategy, don't listen to the rules, and can think only of joining the other kids in the excitement.

Traders usually learn about forex from a friend, at a trading conference, or on the Internet. When they first hear about it, they are excited and will spend a little bit of time getting up to speed on how the market works and maybe even open a practice trading account. However, as they see how active the forex markets can be and the swings in profit and loss that the moves can provide, overly excited traders will quickly abandon their practice accounts and dive right into the market with real money. Oftentimes they do not even have a concrete plan other than to make money. What ends up happening to new traders is the same thing that happens to kids in a funhouse, which is that they will move a few steps forward, run into a few dead-ends that turn into losses, and walk around in a daze until they find the exit. The difference between a funhouse and trading is that the kids will always find the exit—some take longer than others but eventually everyone comes out a happy camper. However, in trading, new traders can exhaust their capital long before they are able to muddle through and find an effective trading strategy.

What separates the professionals from the amateurs is preparation. Professionals such as hedge fund managers or bank traders usually do hours of research and analysis before placing a trade. This includes knowing exactly how much they are willing to risk on any one trade and when they plan to take a profit. Most individuals don't strive to become hedge fund managers but in many ways this type of discipline is even more important to individual traders. Hedge fund managers may be managing millions or billions of dollars—but most of it is other people's money. Individual traders, on the other hand, may only be trading $10,000 or $100,000, but each dollar is their own hard-earned money.

Picking the Right Products

It's important to start properly; the first step is figuring out exactly which forex product, or instrument, is right for you. Investing or trading currencies has become so popular that every few years there are new ways to access the market. The oldest market in the world is called the spot market because transactions are settled "on the spot"; the prices in the spot market determine the price of every other forex instrument including options, futures, forwards, and exchange-traded funds (or ETFs for short).

With so many different ways to tap the market, the first question that you should ask yourself is what am I looking to do? Invest, trade, or hedge? Every forex instrument can be used for these three purposes, but some are more suitable than others.

For investors, ETFs, futures, and spot are the most common ways to take a view on currencies. Exchange-traded funds can usually be bought and sold directly in a stock account with a traditional broker. As with stocks, investors usually buy and hold the ETFs for months. The biggest advantage of investing through ETFs is that the instrument is actually traded on an exchange such as the NYSE, making it easy to track its value. The biggest disadvantage, however, is that liquidity dries up once the stock market closes. Also, the pricing is not as favorable as one would expect from trading the underlying or spot because the execution is not instantaneous, and brokerage fees apply. Yet this is the cost of using an exchange-traded product; many investors are more than willing to pay up for its safety and simplicity, especially if they intend to hold the currency for months. Investing in spot is another option. The spot market provides some of the tightest spreads, but because most accounts are defaulted at high leverage, investors have to specially request lower leverage or consciously allocate only a small portion of their account to the position.

The most popular way for speculators to trade in the forex market is through spot and futures. The spot market is the world's largest market; it has the tightest spreads—more than $4 trillion in daily trading volume—and offers true round-the-clock trading. It is also in the spot market that retail brokers offer leverage as high as 50 to 1 in the United States, which can be an advantage or a disadvantage because leverage magnifies profits and losses. Exhibit 4.1 shows how leverage can impact the profits and losses of a trader who has put up $2,000 at 50 to 1 leverage and no leverage. At 50 times leverage, $2,000 margin controls $100,000 worth of currency. If the position moves

Exhibit 4.1   What Leverage Can Do to Profits and Losses

USD/JPY Rate	50:1 Profit/Loss	No Leverage Profit/Loss
86.50	+$1,734.10	+$34.68
86.00	+$1,162.79	+$23.25
85.50	+$584.79	+$11.69
85.00	$100,000	$2,000
84.50	−$591.71	−$11.83
84.00	−$1,190.48	−$23.81
83.50	−$1,796.41	−$35.93

in the trader's favor, then higher leverage is an advantage, but if moves against him, it becomes a disadvantage.

Like ETFs, forex futures are also traded on an exchange where the market is very liquid and regulated. However, the problem with trading currencies through futures is that the contract sizes are standardized, and unless the investor rolls over the contract every month, it may be subject to physical delivery. Brokerage fees and commissions also apply. Futures margins and account minimums are generally higher and leverage is lower than what is offered by retail forex brokers.

The most common ways to hedge forex risk is through forwards, futures, and options. Forwards are usually done directly with a bank, which means that the amount has to be large enough for a bank to be willing to pick up your phone call and quote you a rate on a customized forward contract where they agree to buy or sell the currency at a specified price on a future date. Futures, on the other hand, are exchange traded so anyone can buy or sell them. Futures are popular for companies that are willing to use standardized amounts, but they may not provide a perfect hedge. Options have limited downside risk and can be bought for a set expiration date. They can be customized for larger transactions and exchange traded for smaller ones. Options are leveraged contracts that usually require a small upfront payment but are subject to time decay.

Over the past few years, hedging forex risk has become very popular among international portfolio managers. However, individuals who hold foreign stock may also want to consider hedging against adverse currency moves; the worst thing that can happen is that the European stock you hold increases 10 percent in value but the euro falls 7 percent in value, erasing nearly all of your equity-related gains.

Trading options, futures, and forex—or any speculative behavior, for that matter—can be risky so make sure you evaluate the instruments properly.

Finding a Broker

Once you understand the A to Zs of forex trading and have decided which instrument is right for you, it is time to pick a broker.

There are many forex brokers and dealers around the world and there is good chance that someone offers forex trading in your hometown. However, just because someone offers forex trading and touts tight spreads doesn't mean they are a reliable broker. When choosing a broker, it may be helpful to consider the following questions:

- How many years has the broker been in business?
- Is the broker regulated and, if so, in how many different countries?
- Are they sufficiently capitalized? (The CFTC publishes this information on their web site for U.S. brokers at www.cftc.gov/MarketReports/FinancialDataforFCMs/index.htm.)
- How many offices do they have? Is there an office in your country?
- Do they provide 24-hour customer and technical support? Can they speak your language?
- Do they provide education?
- Do they offer Web and mobile trading?
- What is the minimum to open an account?
- Does their charting package have all of the features that you need?
- Do they offer real-time news?
- What other value-added services do they offer?

Before deciding on one broker, open demo accounts with a few of them to test their execution and customer service. Speedy and satisfactory responses by customer service and patient platform walkthroughs are usually indicative of a broker that cares about their clients.

Deciding What to Trade

Once you have settled on a broker, it is time to think about what to trade. Most experienced forex traders will use a combination of technical and fundamental analysis. Technical analysis is the art of chart reading and a very popular way to analyze stocks, futures, and commodities. If you are familiar with chart reading, then currencies can basically be analyzed the same way as stocks. The only difference is that volume is not tracked on the forex market because it is traded over the counter and therefore volume-based indicators do not apply.

If you are not familiar with technical analysis, then consider fundamental analysis, which involves trading the big themes or stories in the markets and news releases. For example, you may have an opinion on what the Federal Reserve will do at their monetary policy meeting, and that opinion can be translated into a trade. The same goes for a consumer spending or employment report. Many stock market traders will position ahead of these releases, and if the data is good for the stock market, it should also be good for the currency; if the surprise is large enough, the move will continue. Believe it or not, front-page news can also be traded. Whenever there are elections and the race is close, currencies could fall in value because of the uncertainty. A similar reaction occurs if a natural disaster or disease hits a country.

The basic rule of thumb in currency trading is that in times of uncertainty, investors always sell first and ask questions later. The best thing to do is to lean on your strengths and to trade what you know. Many new traders will focus on trading their local currency if it is one of the actively traded ones because they are on the ground and have an intimate understanding of how the economy is performing.

If you are in it for the long haul and want to be a good trader, it's important to learn both technical and fundamental analysis. There are many books dedicated to teaching technical analysis; one of the most thorough is John Murphy's *Technical Analysis of the Financial Markets*. Fundamentals are important to technical traders because they can determine the overall trend in currencies. Technical analysis, on the other hand, can be used by fundamental traders to identify entry and exit points. Breaking news releases can alter the technical outlook for a currency, while the break of key levels can explain bizarre movements. At a bare minimum, it is important for technical traders to be aware of upcoming news events because range trading ahead of an important news release is an unnecessary risk.

The most important tools that forex traders should become familiar with is the charting package that the forex broker offers, the calendar that lays out upcoming economic reports, and the real-time news applet that provides updates on market movements. These are essential resources that can help you become more in tune with the market and learn what seasoned traders consider important; the great thing is that they are provided free by most foreign exchange brokers.

Get It? Got It? Good!

- If you're looking to make a longer term investment, keep it simple with ETFs.
- Spot forex, where positions can be entered into and exited easily, is extremely popular for forex trading.
- Looking to hedge your risk? Try forwards, futures, and options.
- Don't just settle on the first broker you can find. Survey several brokers to find the best fit and sign up for a demo account or two.
- If you're interested in forex trading for the long haul, learn how to analyze a trade: Fundamental analysis aims to determine overall trends, while technical analysis pinpoints exact entries and exits.

Chapter Five

Movers and Shakers

~

*What Causes Currencies to Go
Up or Down?*

ANOTHER GREAT RIDE AT THE AMUSEMENT PARK is the Pirate Ship. Like a pendulum, the ship moves up and down, first swinging so high in the air that your heart feels like it is flying out of your body and then sinking so fast that your skin feels like it is melting into your face. Thankfully the course of the ride has been charted by the engineers and set into motion by the ride's operators. Currencies, on the other hand, rise and fall in value—not by a predetermined course but by people like us. Of course, it takes a lot of people to move a currency; in fact, it takes millions and sometimes billions of dollars to move it by only 1 percent. Big movements in currencies are usually driven by big stories in the financial markets and the direction of interest rates.

The Big Stories

When it comes to the financial markets, staying on top of the big stories is a critical part of becoming a good trader or investor. Newsworthy events such as the subprime crisis and European sovereign debt crisis can have a major impact on the general sentiment of the market and the demand for a country's currency. These are the triggers for the 10 to 15 percent moves in currencies. The events that can have a profound impact on the value of a currency include but are not limited to the following:

- Potential or actual changes in government
- Economic crisis
- Major announcements by finance ministers and central bankers after G20 meetings
- Intervention by central banks
- Strikes and riots
- Wars and terrorism
- Natural disasters
- Decisions made by government officials

In the past few years alone, there have been numerous stories on the front pages that have affected the forex market, such as the near stalemate elections in the United States and Europe, the surprise resignation of Japanese prime ministers (Japan went through four prime ministers between 2006 and 2010), the ousting of U.K. Prime Minister Gordon Brown and Australian Prime Minister Rudd in 2010, the riots in Thailand, and the swine flu outbreak in Mexico. When a political or social crisis hits a country, currency traders usually sell first and ask questions later because currencies are political as well as economic assets.

Anything that threatens the stability or effectiveness of the government can have an instant impact on the currency. Political events generally trigger a stronger reaction in the currencies of emerging market countries, where political institutions are more fragile, but even in the most developed countries in the world like the United States and the United Kingdom, less serious political problems can still hurt the currency. For example, something as foolish as the Japanese finance minister getting fired after appearing drunk at a G7 meeting caused the Japanese yen to sell off sharply against the U.S. dollar for a good few days. If you are one of those people who love reading the front page of newspapers but your eyes glaze over when you reach the business section, then the prospect of currencies reacting to headline-grabbing events may appeal to you as a trading opportunity.

Political and social developments will affect many different financial instruments, but intervention by central banks is unique to the forex market. When a currency becomes excessively strong or weak, the central bank may feel compelled to intervene directly in the foreign exchange market to change the currency's course. The reason is that the value of a country's currency can have a direct impact on the economy and the competitiveness of local companies. Central banks usually start with verbal intervention, which are threats to intervene and stop the currency from rising or falling—sometimes it works, but often it doesn't. Actions speak much louder than words and therefore physical intervention is much more potent. Central banks physically intervene in the foreign exchange market by buying or selling their currency. The reason intervention is so important is that, on a given day, a currency pair typically moves 100 pips throughout the day but when central banks intervene, the currency can move anywhere from 150 to 300 pips in a matter of minutes. As a result, traders take intervention by central banks very seriously because it can shake out their positions. Sometimes it will even mark the top or bottom for a currency, but usually fundamentals (or the reason for the previous move) eventually catch up to the currency and it resumes its prior trend.

A good example is the Swiss franc. Between October 2008 and March 2009, the franc appreciated rapidly against the euro, hitting a record high in the process. This caused a tremendous amount of anxiety for the Swiss National Bank, which was easing monetary policy to support the country's recovery. On March 12, 2009, the Swiss National Bank decided to intervene in the currency market by selling Swiss francs and buying euros. Their physical intervention drove EUR/CHF, which is a currency that moves an average of 70 pips per day, up more than 500 pips in just a few hours. The power of their intervention effectively kept EUR/CHF from falling any further for the next nine months. However, when the European sovereign debt crisis started to brew, investors sought safety in the low-yielding Swiss franc once again and bought the currency in size. As a result, the Swiss franc not only rose above its previous record high against the euro but another 9 percent. The SNB tried to intervene again in May, which caused EUR/CHF to rally for three days, but eventually fundamentals caught up to the currency and it resumed its slide.

The Direction of Interest Rates

Big stories come and go but interest rates are here to stay. Where interest rates are headed is single-handedly the most important long-term driver for currencies.

Globalization has made it easier for investors to shift money from one country to another in search of a higher yield. Imagine that you are a Japanese investor who is offered a paltry 0.1 percent yield by your local bank. If possible, would you rather put your money in Australia where the interest rate is greater than 4 percent? Most likely your answer is yes.

When a central bank changes its key interest rate, it impacts the borrowing costs of individuals, corporations, and even the government. For businesses, higher rates mean higher borrowing costs, making capital investments less attractive. For individuals, it means higher credit card, car, and mortgage payments, which are aimed at slowing growth. Low interest rates, on the other hand, reduce borrowing costs for businesses and corporations, which encourages spending and capital investment and is usually aimed at boosting growth. Over the long run, high rates tend to moderate economic growth, which is bearish for the economy, but in the short run they tend to be bullish for the currency. When investors move their funds into countries with the highest interest rate, the value of that currency increases.

A good example is Australia. The Reserve Bank of Australia has stunned markets by raising their overnight lending rate five times between October 2009 and June 2010 to one of the highest levels in the developed world. Exhibit 5.1 is a daily chart of the AUD/USD currency

Exhibit 5.1   The Impact of Higher Interest Rates on the AUD/USD Currency Pair

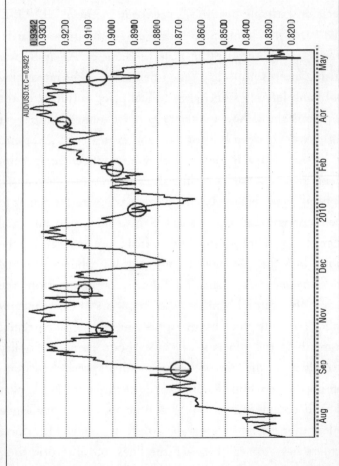

Source: GFT Dealbook 360.

pair with circles highlighting the rate announcements. A closer look at the line chart will also show that the rate decisions usually precede a breakout in the AUD/USD that turns into a multi-day move. The reaction was particularly strong because the Reserve Bank of Australia was raising interest rates at a time when every other major central bank left rates unchanged. The price action after the decisions shows how monetary policy changes can trigger big moves that can last for days and even weeks at a time.

Aside from monetary policy announcements, comments from central bank officials can also move currencies. Central banks hate volatility, particularly when it comes to their currency, so they usually like to telegraph potential changes in interest rates and prepare the market for the move with the aim of reducing volatility when the actual announcement is made. Therefore, comments from the head of the central bank or other members of the monetary policy committee can have a significant impact on currency. Sometimes the officials will talk about monetary policy directly and other times they may only express their opinion on the economy. Knowing the potential market impact of their comments, central bank officials are usually vague unless they intend to telegraph a shift in policy. Therefore, traders have to read between the lines and interpret their message. For example, approximately a week before the Reserve Bank of Australia raised rates in April, Central

Bank Governor Glenn Stevens said that he did not think rates were at "normal levels" yet. The AUD/USD began to rise and, in the end, we learned that his comments were a direct precursor to the 25bp point hike in April.

Day traders, on the other hand, usually trade on the back of economic data, the sentiment in the market, and technical indicators.

Economic Data

The financial media across the world gets very wound up ahead of major economic reports because they know the outcome of the report can set the tone for trading. The same pieces of economic data that move the equity market will move the currency market. Aside from the central bank rate announcement, which can also be traded on an intraday basis, the top three most market-moving economic data for any country are:

- Employment reports
- Retail sales
- Manufacturing and service sector data

Employment Reports.   Labor market data is one of the most important and widest reaching measures of the health of an economy. Just think about it: If you and your neighbor are employed, both of you are more likely to spend, but if your neighbor gets laid off and some of your other friends are let go as well, there is a good chance that all of you will cut back spending. In most industrialized nations, consumer spending is the engine for growth. When the job market is strong and companies are hiring, there is more money being shuffled around, translating into greater spending and ultimately higher growth; that is generally positive for the country's currency. On the other hand, if companies are cutting jobs left and right, it is a sign that the economy is slowing down, which can hurt the currency. In the United States, the employment report is called the Non-Farm Payrolls report; when this piece of economic data is released, it can trigger a very big reaction in the EUR/USD. Typically the EUR/USD fluctuates within a 100- to 150-pip range on a daily basis but when the Non-Farm Payrolls report is released, the EUR/USD can move 100 pips in one or two hours.

Retail Sales.   While the employment report tells how consumer spending could fare, the retail sales and consumption reports tell us how consumers actually behaved. The employment report is usually released before the retail sales report, which is why it can have a greater impact on the market. Strong consumer spending usually means an economy is improving or growing (that's good for the currency!) whereas weak consumer spending usually means an economy is declining or slowing down (not so good for the currency). When consumers start to spend less, companies start to produce less, which can lead to cutbacks on hiring and spending.

Manufacturing and Services Data.   The robustness of manufacturing and services sector activity is very important to the economic growth of a country because manufacturing and services make up the economy. These reports are released before employment reports and can signal potential layoffs or hiring. The reports are typically known as the Purchasing Managers Index, but in the United States they are referred to as the Institute for Supply Management Report. These releases track activity on a scale from 0 to 100. A number above 50 indicates expansion and growth, while a number below 50 is a signal of economic contraction. A stronger expansion usually leads to gains in the currency, while a weaker expansion usually leads to currency weakness.

Traders have to be particularly careful when trading news because when large surprises emerge, sharp movements can occur, which makes it extremely important to limit your exposure and manage your risk.

Market Sentiment

Day traders also depend on market sentiment more than swing traders. Since currencies and equities react to the same things, it should not be surprising that the two markets move in lockstep. If there is no news or economic data released, the currency market will take its cue from stocks, particularly if the Dow Jones Industrial Average or other indices are moving significantly. On a day-to-day basis, risk appetite or the nervousness of investors often dictates how currencies will trade. If stocks are rallying, it generally means that traders are optimistic and willing to take on risk, which is positive for high-yielding currencies. If stocks are down materially, that is usually synonymous with risk aversion, which encourages forex traders to seek safety in low-yielding currencies and reduce exposure to high-yielding ones.

Technicals Matter, Too

Lastly, day traders have a soft spot for technical analysis. Technical analysis or chart reading is another popular way to pinpoint entry and exit levels in currencies. Chapters 6 through 9 explain just how that can be done. The break of important prices can cause sharp movements in currencies during quiet times when there are no economic reports or news releases. Many trading orders such as stops and limits are set at round numbers for the same reasons we celebrate our 10th and 20th wedding anniversaries and not our 9th and 19th anniversaries—because they are psychologically palatable levels. The most common places to put orders are at round numbers and at 50 pip increments—the more zeros, the better. This means that 100.00 or 1.1000 is a level at which many traders, investors, and companies that are hedging will place orders. A round number is basically a price level where the last two decimal points are zeros—so 105.00 is a round number as well as 1.0200. Every 100-pip increment will attract stops, and a break of those levels can trigger a sharp burst in price action as brokers process orders that either get their clients into new positions or out of old ones.

Aside from the big stories, the direction of interest rates, economic data, stocks, and technicals, other factors such as option expirations, mergers, and acquisitions of companies can also trigger small blips in price action. However, their impact is generally small and does not last, so if you hear these terms used to explain price movements, don't worry about them because they are not generally sustainable.

Knowing what moves currencies is important but this does not necessarily help traders determine where to enter and exit their trades, the biggest mystery of trading. There are many different ways to trade currencies on an intraday or swing basis. The next chapter will introduce some super simple strategies and tools to make it easier to identify your next great trade.

Get It? Got It? Good!

- If an event is big enough to take up space on page 1 of your newspaper, it's big enough to impact your trading. Consider these events when placing a trade.
- When there's news of political instability, currency traders usually sell first and ask questions later.
- The most important long-term driver for currencies is interest rates. Whether rates are going up, going down, or stuck like glue, it means something.
- Listen to central bank officials. What they say can impact currencies.
- Know when countries are releasing economic data or reports and be ready to trade.
- Chart reading (also known as technical analysis) is a good way to find your way into a trade. Remember, people love to put their orders near round numbers.

Chapter Six

The Investor versus the Trader

*Finding the Right
Approach for You*

OVER THE NEXT FEW CHAPTERS, WE SPEND PLENTY of time talking about trading tactics and strategies, but first let me introduce to you my dear friends Andrew and Steven, whose polar opposite personalities can teach us a great deal about how we should approach the forex market. There are a million different ways to trade currencies— some involve holding onto a position for a few minutes while others involve holding it for days. Both strategies can be effective if the person who implements it (yes, YOU) is the right person for the job.

Meet Andrew and Steven

Andrew and Steven are brothers who live in New York City. Steven is a dentist with a thriving practice in downtown Manhattan. He has two beautiful daughters with perfect teeth and impeccable manners. Andrew, who is three years younger, is a talented architect with his own business that focuses on servicing small-property developers. Both brothers are diehard Yankees fans who share a passion for golf and all things made by Steve Jobs, but when it comes to investing, they could not be any more different.

Being a dentist who makes a very good living drilling teeth, Steven needs to work only 35 to 40 hours a week. His 10-hour days are as long as most people's, but his practice is open only four days a week. The rest of the time, Steven plays golf, fiddles with his large number of iPad apps, and manages his investments. With a great deal of spare time between patients and workdays, he often instant messages me about his trades and investment ideas. As a devout Mac fanatic, his favorite stock is, of course, Apple. I have long advised Steven to stick with what he knows and so he usually focuses on trading the stocks of medical supply companies and Apple. Although most people would think that dentists are extremely patient, my friend Steven is not. Over the course of a week, he may buy and sell Apple a number of times on both the long and short side. Usually it is ahead of earnings announcements, product releases, or the annual World Wide Developers Conference. Whenever there is a rumor about what Apple may or may not do, such as offering the iPhone through Verizon, Steven is always on top of the news and has an opinion. However, as well as Steven may know Apple and its current and future product offerings, he always ends up selling too early and buying too late. To his credit, he still returned more than 65 percent on his money in 2009 and 2010.

Andrew, on the other hand, works 60 to 70 hours a week. He has no kids but has a few investment properties that he is always doing handiwork on and volunteers often to tutor underprivileged kids in the Bronx. Like Steven, he has a Mac at home and at work, an iPhone, a Shuffle for the gym, and an iPad for his other miscellaneous activities. Andrew also believes that Apple will one day rule the world and every household will have some invention made by Steve Jobs. However, he does not have the same amount of spare time as Steven has to stare at his trading screen and visit CNET, MacRumors, and Engadget multiple times a day. He has held Apple stock since the beginning of 2007 and added small amounts whenever he is paid for an architectural project. By mid-2010, the value of his Apple shares has more than doubled. He has far fewer gray hairs than Steven and not only because he is younger!

One time Steven picked me up in his blue BMW and as we were driving up Sixth Avenue to pick up a cake for a daughter's birthday; a taxicab, trying to switch lanes to pick up a passenger cut us off, causing Steven to slam on his brakes and curse violently. That moment is characteristically Steven, meaning that he can be hotheaded and impatient. Therefore, it should not come as a surprise that he is unable to hold a position in a stock for much longer than a few hours because he spends much of his free time staring at his trading screen, reacting emotionally to each and every half-point move for or against him. In fact, Steven's office is next to his patients' rooms and sometimes when he is waiting on his assistants to do preparatory work, he will run back and forth to check on his trades.

Andrew is the complete opposite of Steven. He is very Zen when it comes to both driving and trading. In New York, getting cut off by other cars is a part of life. In fact, New York drivers have to avoid cars, pedestrians jaywalking, skaters, and bicyclists—it is almost like navigating a safari. Whenever a car cuts Andrew off, he calmly presses on the brakes, barely reacts, and continues to drive. As a long-standing yoga practitioner, he is the epitome of patience. This made me realize that the difference in

Andrew's and Steven's investment behaviors may be partly due to their amount of spare time and partly to their personalities. Impatient Steven is much more of a trader while Zen-like Andrew only cares to be an investor.

Despite their different temperaments, both Steven and Andrew have done a fantastic job of managing their investment portfolios. Books such as Jack D. Schwager's *Market Wizards* (New York Institute of Finance, 1989; Harper's Business, 1993) and *Millionaire Traders: How Everyday People Beat Wall Street at Its Own Game* (John Wiley & Sons, 2007), which I wrote with Boris Schlossberg, have featured very successful traders who have diametrically opposite approaches to the market. The secret to trading is as much in the strategy as it is in the psychology. Successful traders do not fit their personalities to their trading activities but rather find trading approaches that are in line with their personalities. If you have ever tried to trade long term but cringed at every 10th of a percent move against you, then it is time to realize that long-term trading is probably not right for you. At the same time, if you can only check your trading screen once a day and cannot get up early to trade active market hours, then longer term or swing trading may be more suitable for you. Many people have traded successfully on the short or long term—the decision to become a trader or an investor should be determined by your own personality and time.

QUIZ: INSTANT GRATIFICATION OR WILLING TO WAIT?

Here is a quick quiz to help you decide whether trading or investing is right for you.

What do you do when Apple releases a brand-new iPhone? Your choices are:

A. Get up at 4 A.M. on a Saturday morning and wait hours on line in the hot sun to get your hands on the new iPhone the day it is released.

B. Order the iPhone online and wait three weeks for it to arrive.

If you picked A, it means that you have more of a trading mind-set because you seek instant gratification and are willing to pay the price of waiting hours on line in the heat begging someone to hold your space in line during bathroom breaks to get your hands on Apple's latest gadget.

If you chose B, you are likely to be more long term–oriented and are willing to delay your desire for fast cash in order to live a less-demanding lifestyle.

The Waiting Game of Taxi Drivers

We can also learn a lot about trading from the personalities of taxicab drivers. Living in New York City, I take taxis frequently and have always been fascinated by the different choices made by taxi drivers. A taxi medallion, which is an aluminum cap that is bolted to the hood of each cab and gives the drivers the right to operate the taxi, is the priciest piece of aluminum in New York City. The cost of an individual medallion is a jaw-dropping $588,000, while a company-owned medallion costs nearly $780,000. Calling this overpriced would be an understatement, particularly since the corporate medallion only cost $339,000 in 2004. When they were introduced in the 1930s, the cost per medallion was only $10. It has one of the best bull markets with the most consistent returns. Why are medallions so expensive? They are limited and have provided annual returns between 15 and 20 percent, even during the global financial crisis. This staggering price should make you wonder how in the world can an average taxi driver afford to pay for the right to operate a cab—and the answer is that most of them can't. Owners of taxi medallions usually rent out their medallions for as much as $800 per week for one shift. For the poor taxi driver, this means that in order to turn a profit each night, he or she needs to pick up more than $115 in fares and tips. This explains why taxi drivers are so aggressive, cutting off buses and cars driven by people like Steven and Andrew.

However, not all taxi drivers choose to dart around the city looking for a fare. If you have ever flown into a New York City airport, you may have seen hundreds of cabs waiting in the taxi holding area for the dispatcher to release them. The wait is usually between two and three hours. You might be asking why some taxi drivers who have rented out a 12-hour shift are willing to waste hours in a line instead of darting around the city picking up different passengers. The answer is personality and patience.

According to the American Master Cabbie Taxi Academy, which conducts weekly surveys of the income of taxi drivers, the average amount that a full-time night shift driver pulls in per week is approximately $1,000. The income of a daytime driver is slightly less. Assuming that taxi drivers work seven days a week and most of them have to, it puts their daily income at approximately $143. A typical cab ride within the city costs $12 to $15 before tips and $15 to $18 with tips. This means that a taxi driver darting around the city needs to pick up at least nine people to make $140 per day. A cab ride from JFK airport to the city has a flat rate of $45; with tips and toll it usually comes to $60. This means that the taxi driver only needs to pick up two airport fares and one to two city fares to make $140—not only is this less work, but it also saves gas. However, if all taxi drivers just waited at the airport, there would be no cabs in the city. The reason some drivers wait and others don't boils down to patience and the need for instant gratification. Some taxi drivers will sit around for hours waiting for the best fares while others will speed down New York City streets trying to pick up as many lower value fares as possible.

In many ways the psychology of traders is very similar to that of taxi drivers. There are traders who prefer to hang out and wait for the perfect opportunity and others who cannot resist being in the market and participating even if it means smaller profits.

Are You Jack Shephard or John Locke?

One of the most popular TV shows of the twenty-first century is *Lost*. The essence of *Lost* is that a band of people constantly operates in a highly dangerous environment without any helpful information. In short, every character must make life-or-death decisions with imperfect knowledge of the situation at hand. No one exemplifies this idea better than Locke. Not the new "smoky" Locke played with great malevolence by Terry O'Quinn, but the old, bumbling John Locke who is always trying to do the right thing but inevitably ends up making the wrong decision. The old Locke is presented as a man of faith who is ultimately a follower; he is juxtaposed with Jack Shephard's man of reason who questions everything he is confronted with. Jack and John are the quintessential examples of two types of traders—faders and followers.

The Jack Shephards of the world are the faders and contrarians who question everything they are confronted with. If Jack were a trader, he would probably look at every 1 percent drop in the EUR/USD as a better opportunity to buy in anticipation of a bottom. The John Lockes and the followers of the world would probably ride a move until there is a sign that tells him that it is time to change. If Locke were a trader and the EUR/USD was selling off, he would probably sell the currency pair until it finally reverses. Skeptics and contrarians are more suited for range trading because, as much as Locke may try to get Jack to see his ways, he simply can't. For everyone else, trend following is probably more appropriate since it is the stronger dynamic in the forex market. Neither of these tactics are wrong—they are just two different approaches to the market suitable for traders with different personalities.

To new traders, this idea of determining your trading style based upon your personality may seem completely illogical, but the real point is to stick with your strengths. Would it have been smart for Babe Ruth, one of baseball's most prolific hitters, to return to pitching? Should Mario Batali, one of America's best Italian chefs, hinge his career and savings on a Chinese restaurant? Should Tiger Woods try his chance on "Dancing with the Stars"? Probably not. Although they could have become successful, the foundation of their careers should be rooted in what they know and do best.

My colleague Boris Schlossberg said it well in his book *Technical Analysis of the Currency Market*:

> The cold hard truth of life is that we do not really change; we just grow older. The most successful businesspeople in the world learn how to utilize their strengths while minimizing their weaknesses by having their more skilled colleagues perform those tasks, which they cannot do well. Trading is very much the same. Successful traders choose those strategies that are most aligned with their psychological profiles while staying out of the market when conditions aren't suitable for their style. It isn't a matter of doing the easy thing or the difficult thing. All trading is difficult. Rather it's a matter of doing the natural thing. Why is this concept so important? Couldn't you simply learn proper trading habits with enough practice and discipline? No. No matter how much discipline you possess, if you are trading contrary to your natural impulses you will eventually sabotage your trading plan and you will fail.

When trying to figure out which type of trading style is right for you, keep in mind that short and long term in the forex market is very different from short and long term in the stock market because leverage magnifies profits and losses.

Short-term currency traders generally hold their positions for only a few minutes, a few hours, or a few days. Any longer and it would be considered an investment. A position held for a few minutes or hours is typically called a day trade, while a position held for a few days or at most a few weeks is referred to as a swing trade. Day and swing traders approach the market in very different ways. Swing traders look to latch onto themes in the market that can turn into multiday moves, while day traders like to take advantage of small bursts in price movements.

Get It? Got It? Good!

- Being a good trader is about finding the right strategy that fits your personality.
- We're all adults. Don't expect to easily mold your personality to a trading style.
- If you don't have much patience, you might be best suited to day trading.
- If you don't mind waiting it out, you might be best suited for medium-term trading or something bordering on investing.
- Short- and long-term trading in the forex market is very different from short- and long-term trading in the stock market; remember, leverage magnifies profits and losses.

Chapter Seven

What All Winners Do

~

*Must-Follow Rules for
Everyone in Forex*

SUCCESSFUL PEOPLE USUALLY HAVE A FEW COMMON traits—
such as being a hard worker and forward thinker. So it
shouldn't surprise you that the people who have invested
or traded successfully in the forex market also have a few
things in common. I talk to profitable and unprofitable
traders on a regular basis and here are some tips drawn
from their experience and mine that will benefit everyone—
regardless of whether you are an investor or trader.

Everyone talks about the value of following the trend, but almost no one actually does it. This is one of the great ironies of forex trading. So how *are* potential profits made?

Katz's Delicatessen is a New York institution that has been selling the most delectable pastrami sandwiches since 1888. Both locals and tourists pack the restaurant night and day for a taste of their famous juicy black pepper–coated pastrami. In 1990, a pastrami sandwich cost approximately $7.50. By 2010, the price had more than doubled. So how was Katz's able to double their prices and still keep customers? It's because they have always had a sufficient number of buyers.

Profits are made in trading when the majority of the market is on the side of your position. If you are long, the price moves up when there are more buyers; if you are short, the price moves down when there are more sellers. The more people that favor your trade, the more likely it will continue to move in your favor, and the more money you could potentially make. By instinct, many people choose to go against the grain and pick tops and bottoms. Surprisingly, it is rarely a question of value and mostly just a matter of ego. Every time we fade, we say, "I know better! You, Mr. Market, are wrong! I'm smarter than you and will not follow you like all the rest of these suckers!" When we are right, the feeling is intoxicating, but when we are wrong, the results can be debilitating. The secret of forex trading is to give yourself the greatest edge possible by staying with the trend, bagging your winners quickly, and knowing when to say no.

Stay with the Trend

In the first few chapters of this book, we went into great length about why currencies spend more time in trend than in range. (A range is defined as the high and low of a currency pair; when a currency trades in a range, it remains within certain highs and lows. In a trend, on the other hand, we usually see a currency pair make new highs or new lows.) Pull up any weekly or monthly chart of the EUR/USD and you will see that for the past 10 years, there have been more months where the EUR/USD continued its prior move than it has reversed it. How currencies behave reflect how investors feel about the country's economic outlook; the economy of a country typically gets progressively better or progressively worse with time.

Take the EUR/USD, for example. Exhibit 7.1 shows how the EUR/USD traded between 2006 and the first half of 2010. In the first few months of 2010, the EUR/USD fell six months in a row. Between June and October 2009, the EUR/USD rose for five months straight. In 2008, the EUR/USD made consecutive monthly lows for only four months, but in that period the currency pair lost more than 20 percent.

Exhibit 7.1   A EUR/USD Trend Can Last for Months

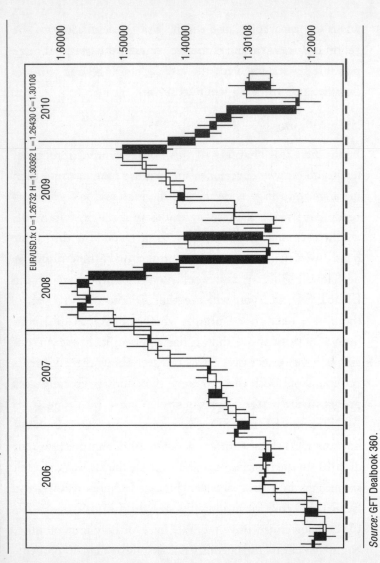

Source: GFT Dealbook 360.

In 2006 and 2007, the trend was even more obvious. Although weekly and daily charts will show areas where profits can be made from reversals, the greater and less stressful opportunities were in the direction of the trend.

In the EUR/USD's move from a high of 1.50 in November 2009 to 1.19 by June 2010, 1.45, 1.40, 1.30, 1.25, and 1.20 all looked like good value points. Eventually 1.19 was the best place to buy, but tops and bottoms are only obvious in hindsight. Yogi Berra had something to say about that.

Predicting is very hard, especially about the future.

If Sir John Templeton traded currencies, he would have probably waited until the moves became extreme and the valuation was off the charts (either under- or overvalued) before picking a top or bottom. But unless you have extremely deep pockets like Templeton, you may not be able to sit with a trade and wait for the currency to finally turn around. Most contrarians like Templeton and even some traders like John Paulson, who started to position for a subprime crisis in 2006, have had to sit with their losing positions for weeks, months, and sometimes years on the hope that they will capture most of their profits in one single period of collapse. Paulson made billions doing just that, but beneath the glamour, he fought against significant skepticism from his peers who believed that it was too dangerous to bank the entire fund on one single bet that would be difficult to unwind. Eventually Paulson's bet paid off handsomely but not until a year later.

Most currency traders simply do not have the luxury of deep pockets and time. Forex brokers offer as much as 50 to 1 leverage, and even on a very modest 10 to 1 leverage, a mere 10 percent negative move will wipe out the entire account. Paulson believed that his investors would be willing to lose 8 percent a year on mortgage insurance for the opportunity to earn a lot more. However, 8 percent for a regular currency speculator on a 10 to 1 lever factor can be debilitating.

So how can you tell when a currency is trending? There are many different ways to determine when a currency is in trend. One of the most popular is to use a combination of the Average Directional Index (ADX) and moving averages. The ADX is a fancy indicator created by an incredibly intelligent man named J. Welles Wilder and is used to evaluate the strength of a trend. When the ADX reading is greater than 25 and pointing upward, it signals that the currency pair is in trend and the trend is strengthening. If the ADX is falling, it usually implies that the prior trend is exhausting and by the time it dips back below 25, the currency pair is most likely range trading. Moving averages measure the momentum of a move and are used to determine the direction of the trend. If the currency pair is trading comfortably above the moving average, then it means it is in an uptrend. If it is trading well below the moving average, then it means it is in a downtrend.

Exhibit 7.2 shows a weekly chart of the EUR/USD and how the ADX and moving average can be used together to determine when a currency pair has begun to trend. The up arrows in the chart point to when the trend begins and the down arrows point to when the trend ends, according to the ADX. Remember, ADX above 25 and pointing upward signals trend and ADX below 25 *or* pointing downward signals exhaustion or range. The moving average helps to determine the direction of the trend. Taking a look at the very first signal on the left, we can see that the ADX effectively signaled the beginning and end of the uptrend (because the currency pair was trading above the 20 period moving average). The same is true for the other examples in the chart. The only problem is that the ADX can give a late signal, as it did in the last two examples, and it does not always provide effective entry and exit points.

Another good option is to use Double Bollinger Bands to determine whether a currency pair is in trend. In Exhibit 7.3, arrows show the ADX signals while the

Exhibit 7.2   Joining the Trend Using Average Directional Index (ADX) Signals

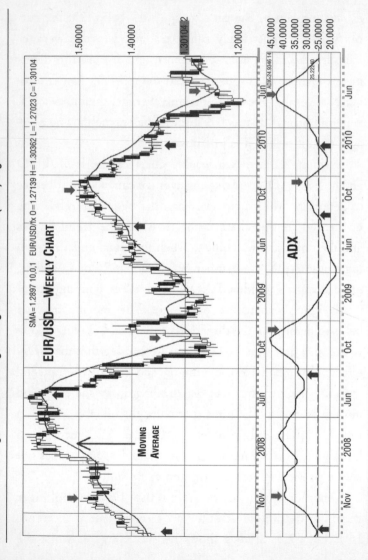

Exhibit 7.3 Joining the Trend Using Bollinger Bands

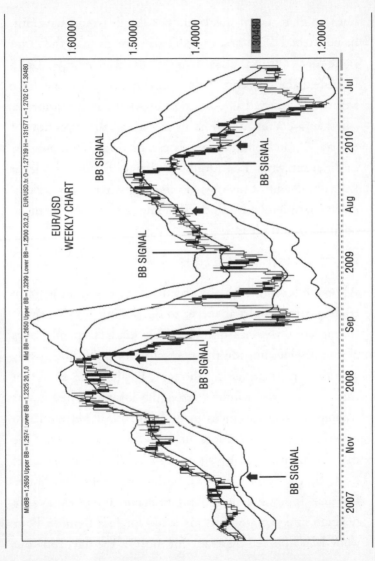

MidBB = 1.2650 Upper BB = 1.297: .ower BB = 1.2325 20,1,0   Mid BB = 1.2650 Upper BB = 1.2900 20,2,0   EUR/USD.fx O = 1.27139 H =1.31577 L = 1.2702 C = 1.30480

1.60000

1.50000

1.40000

1.30480

1.20000

EUR/USD
WEEKLY CHART

BB SIGNAL

BB SIGNAL

BB SIGNAL

BB SIGNAL

BB SIGNAL

2007   Nov   2008   Sep   2009   Aug   2010   Jul

Source: GFT Dealbook 360.

lines point to when the Bollinger Bands would have signaled a trend. The first two signals were given at the exact same time, but in the last two signals, the Bollinger Band identified the currency pair as moving into a trend long before the ADX. In addition to providing information on whether a currency pair is in trend and the direction of the trend, the Bollinger Bands can be traded in a number of different ways. The Double Bollinger Bands are such a key component of my own trading that Chapter 8 is dedicated completely to understanding and using them to position into trades.

Bag Your Winners Quickly

Although staying with the trend will give you an edge in trading forex, the real secret to developing consistency is to bag your winners quickly. Most traders spend hours and hours looking for the perfect entry point and barely give their exits a passing thought, but it is the exits that can separate the winners from the losers. When I was trading at a major investment bank, I sat between two experienced forex traders named Tom and Masa. One day, they went long and short the EUR/USD at the exact time. By the end of the day, both were profitable. Why? Because Tom was only looking to make 20 pips on a large position and remained in his trade for less than an hour while Masa nursed his trade for most of the day, rode out the initial losses and waited for the currency to turn around and hit his profit target of 50 pips. The entry in this case did not matter at all because Tom and Masa took opposing positions at the exact same time. Instead, what made them both winners was their exit.

In Trading or Investing 101, all of us are taught to maintain a strict 2 to 1 risk/reward ratio or better. In other words, for every $100 risked, we need to look to make $200. The reason is that we need to be right only 50 percent of the time to be net positive and even less if the risk/reward ratio is higher. For example, if you had a trading strategy that risked 50 points for a return of 150 points on every trade, you would only need to be successful 30 percent of the time to be net positive. In other words, if 7 out of 10 trades were losers and 3 were winners, the net return would still be 100 points. Sounds attractive, right?

The standard trading advice is to have your winners be much larger than your losers, but anyone who has traded currencies has most likely experienced the frustration of watching the trade turn profitable, but for one reason or another, the profits start to disappear like ice cubes in your hand and eventually turn into a losing trade. The problem is that markets are generally not that generous, and for some traders, 2 to 1 risk/reward ratios may be ideal but not realistic.

Imagine a short-term trader who is only looking to risk 35 pips on a given trade. To keep with a strict 2:1 ratio, he would need to make 70 pips on the trade. However, on any given day, a currency pair only moves an average of 100 pips, which means that in the isolated amount of time that he is available to monitor the trade, he is looking to make 70 percent of an average day's move. Another possible scenario is that our trader plans to make 20 pips per trade. Under a 2:1 ratio, he needs to set his stop at 10 pips. However a 10-pip stop can be clipped at the blink of an eye, particularly since the spread reduces the stop by 2 to 3 pips, depending upon which currency is traded.

An overly ideal risk to reward ratio encourages traders to try and take more from the market than is being offered and may encourage scalpers to use excessively tight stops. So how do you overcome this? By using the T1-T2 method.

To minimize the risk of letting profits melt in their hands like ice cubes on a hot sunny day, many professional traders like to bag their winners quickly using a T1-T2 method to exit of their trades. T1 simply refers to Target 1 and T2 refers to Target 2. Not only have I met many traders who say that the T1-T2 method has transformed their returns but I use this methodology in my own trading. The idea is to have a conservative, relatively easy-to-achieve first target and a more ambitious second target. So if I am looking to risk 40 pips on my trade, my first target should be approximately 40 pips. In order for me to be net positive, my strategy needs to hit 60 to 70 percent more winners than losers. However, with a smaller first target of 40 pips, the chances of the limit being reached can be greater than a target of 70 pips. When the target is hit, I would close out half of the position and move my stop to breakeven on the remainder of the position. The idea is to limit your losses to your initial entry point. If the trade continues to move in my favor, then I will trail the stop to lock in more profits. If the trade moves backwards to stop me out at my initial entry price, which is known as breakeven, the overall trade would still be a positive one because I banked profits on the first half of the position.

Why does this work? We have all heard the statement that 20 percent of employees generate 80 percent of a company's output and 20 percent of customers provide 80 percent of the revenue. To some degree, the same as true in trading. Trends can be strong and it is important to try to capture as much of a trend move as possible, while at the same time limiting your risk. Floating profits are just that—floating. They can hit an iceberg anytime, which is why I believe it is much better to take partial profits early and try to ride the rest to glory with only a part of the position. When it comes to trading, a bird in the hand *is* worth two in the bush.

Human psychology is also a big reason why the T1-T2 method works well for many traders. My business partner, Boris Schlossberg, posed a very good question to make an important point to our clients: "Suppose I gave you a choice. You can take ten trades, nine of which would lose you $10,000 each or $90,000 in total and the tenth would make you $120,000 for a net profit of $30,000. Or you can take ten trades of which seven would make you $20,000 each and three would lose you $40,000 each for a net profit of $20,000. Which would you prefer?"

On the surface the first strategy appears to make you more money but 90 percent of traders will most likely wind up losers under that method. Why? Human beings hate to lose. Furthermore, they hate to lose consistently. If you deconstruct the first strategy, you basically have only 1 out of 10 chances to make a winning trade. These are lottery-like odds for an average trader. Here is what's most likely to happen: You will quit after the third trade and never catch the winning trade in the sequence. You will cut your winning trade short because you are so desperate to recoup some—any—part of your money that the end result will still end up negative. Or worst of all, you will miss the one winning trade and will simply generate nine losers in your account.

Flip the scenarios. In strategy number two, you have 7 out of 10 chances to win. That fact alone is likely to keep you on track and help you adhere to your trading strategy. Furthermore, if you are lucky, you may even miss one of the large losers and improve your performance even more. That's the paradox of negative edge.

We trade with a negative edge not because we think it is mathematically superior—we know that it is not. In fact, in order for the T1-T2 method to work, our strategy needs to be successful at least 60 to 70 percent of the time because trading more than one lot doubles the losers. We trade with negative edge because we know that it is psychologically more palatable, and trading at its core is always more psychological than it is logical. Academics never factor in human frailty as a variable and yet it is perhaps the most important element in achieving long-term trading success.

Know When to Say No

Finally the third trading edge is to know when to walk away. When trading with trend, chasing price is probably one of the most dangerous things that you can do. If you have ever been involved in a bidding war on eBay and regretted it because you ended up paying twice the retail price for some piece of secondhand garbage, you will know how it can get you in trouble. There will always be another trade, so know when to say NO.

Get It? Got It? Good!

- Currency trends can be very strong, so try to find trades in the direction of the trend.
- Throw out the notion of only following risk to reward ratios of 2:1 because they are not always realistic!
- Don't let your winners turn into losers. Bank some profits early in increments and use a smaller part of your position to participate in the trend.
- If the trend has become overextended, avoid chasing the price move. That will only increase your risk of being stopped out.

Chapter Eight

So You're an Investor?

~

Slow and Steady Wins the Race

LIKE A LOCOMOTIVE THAT IS SLOWLY TRAVELING from one part of a country to another, slow and steady investing is about taking things easy—enjoying the ride and not stressing about the time it takes to get where you're going. Chapter 6 talked about how investing in the forex market is slightly different from investing in the stock market. The high amount of leverage available to forex traders magnifies profits and losses, which is why the holding period of currency investments tends to be shorter than that of equity investments. In this chapter, we will talk about different ways to join moves that last for weeks.

One of the most memorable moments in my career was when John Bollinger, the mastermind and namesake behind Bollinger Bands, stood behind a crowd and watched me show traders in Singapore the Double Bollinger Bands. He said to one of my colleagues that it was a "clever way to use the bands." Of the hundreds of technical indicators out there, the Double Bollinger Bands are hands down my favorite. Through the years, the bands have become a critical component of my trading. The reason I really love the Double Bollinger Bands (BB bands for short) is they provide a wealth of actionable information. They tell me whether a currency pair is in trend or range, the direction of the trend, and when the trend has exhausted. More importantly, Bollinger Bands also identify entry points and proper places to put a stop.

Bollinger Band Basics

Before describing how the Double Bollinger Bands work, it is important to first explain them. Bollinger Bands consists of three lines—a 20-period moving average, which is the center line and then the upper and lower lines, which are basically a specific standard deviation away from the moving average. Just imagine a two-lane highway with a center divider that is the moving average and barriers on either side, which are the standard deviations.

The default Bollinger Band parameters on most charting packages are 20 periods and two standard deviations. Although understanding the math behind how the bands are created may be complicated for some, the way they are used is more important and simple to grasp.

The purpose of the bands is to determine how high or low a currency pair has moved in relation to the average price over the past 20 periods. Two standard deviations is considered quite rare because in Statistics 101, it is said that 95 percent of all activity should fall within two standard deviations of the average and only 5 percent should fall outside of that amount. Applying this to currencies means that when the currency pair reaches the second standard deviation band, the move has hit an extreme point because the idea is that 95 percent of the time the currency pair trades between the bands. However, the problem with this notion is that a quick look at currency charts overlaid with Bollinger Bands will show that reaching the extremes happens more often than we would think. We know that currencies can move in one direction for a long period of time and there will be times when it may touch the Bollinger Band five days in a row, making a rare event a common occasion. This is why we devised the Double Bollinger Band Method, which we have found to be a much better use of Bollinger's creation.

The Double Bollinger Band Method consists of using two sets of Bollinger Bands. In addition to the second standard deviation Bollinger Band just mentioned, we also use a first deviation Bollinger Band. The centerlines (or medians) are excluded because otherwise the charts become very messy and crowded. Exhibit 8.1 shows how the Bollinger Bands would look on a daily chart of USD/JPY. The two outside lines are the second standard deviation Bollinger Bands and the two inside lines are the first standard deviation Bollinger Bands. Once the Double Bollinger Bands are set up, they can be used for identifying whether the currency is in a range or trend, if and when a trend has exhausted, where to find value within the trend, and how to get into a new trend.

The most important thing that the Double Bollinger Bands do is answer the $500 million question of whether the currency pair is in trend or range. When a trend is very strong, most of the currency pair's price action will be confined within the one and two standard deviation Bollinger Bands. The Double Bollinger Bands also determine the direction of the trend. The two bands at the lower part of the chart capture the downtrend while the two bands at the upper part of the chart capture the uptrend.

In other words, if the USD/JPY was trading between the upper one and two standard deviation bands, it is in

Exhibit 8.1   Using Double Bollinger Bands with USD/JPY

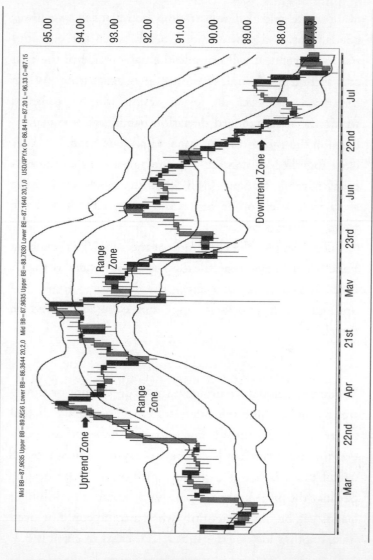

Mid BB = 87.9635 Upper BB = 89.5EC6 Lower BB = 86.3644 20,2.0   Mid 3B = 87.9635 Upper BE = 88.7630 Lower BE = 87.1640 20,1.0   USD/JPY.fx O = 86.84 H = 87.20 L = 96.33 C = 87.15

Source: GFT Dealbook 360.

[109]

an uptrend, and if it was trading between the two lower bands, it is in a downtrend. Usually when the currency pair is in trend, it will not end the day outside of the first and second bands unless the trend is exhausting. When the trend is weak, the price action will be confined within the first standard deviation bands (the two center-lines) in the range-trading zone. If all four bands are very close together, we can see with the naked eye that the currency is range trading. Only when the bands are moving away from each other or are far apart already will the trend indicators be useful.

For example, the right side of the USD/JPY chart in Exhibit 8.1 shows that during the move from 90 to 87, USD/JPY never traded above the downtrend zone. The uptrend, downtrend, and range zones are all marked on the chart.

Knowing When the Trend Has Exhausted

When the currency pair moves outside the up- or down-trend zone and into the range-trading zone, it signals that the trend has exhausted. For bottom-fishers and top pickers, the Bollinger Bands can be an easy-to-understand and useful tool. Rather than blindly picking a top or bottom because the price looked expensive or cheap, the Bollinger Bands can be used to identify when a trend could be over. Take another look at the USD/JPY chart in Exhibit 8.1.

You may notice that when USD/JPY falls out of the uptrend zone, the move will frequently extend to the lower first standard deviation Bollinger Band. In contrast, if USD/JPY rises out of the downtrend zone, the rally will frequently extend to the upper first standard deviation Bollinger Band. It does not happen 100 percent of the time, but enough to make it meaningful. Therefore, if USD/JPY has been falling and trading within the downtrend zone, a practical way to pick a bottom would be to wait for the currency pair to close above the lower first standard deviation Bollinger Band with a stop at the most significant near-term low. Although the upper first standard deviation Bollinger Band could be a target, usually it is a few hundred pips away. Instead it would be smarter to apply the T1-T2 method, which involves taking off half of the position when the profits have reached a reasonable amount and then trailing your stop on the rest of the position. If you overlaid a 15-period moving average onto the chart, you can see that most turns will reach the 15-period Simple Moving Average, which could be used as a place to exit the first part of your position.

Finding Value within a Trend

The difficulty that most traders have with following trends is finding a proper place to enter. When trends are very strong, the moves can be very deep; if you missed entering the trade when the trend first began, you could wind up buying the high or selling the low. Chasing a trade can be dangerous because it also exposes the position to retrace risk, which occurs when a currency pair rebounds slightly after selling off aggressively (a common occurrence) by just enough to stop you out and still remain within a downtrend. Jumping into a trend when the momentum is at its strongest also makes it very difficult to place a technically significant stop at a reasonable rate. To resolve this problem, we use the Double Bollinger Bands to find value within a trend. The idea is to basically wait for a bargain before buying because, as our coupon-clipping grandmothers will tell us, it is always better to pay a discount than to pay a premium.

Instead of entering a trade at any random point simply because we want to participate in the move, it is generally better to wait for the currency pair to "retrace" to the first standard deviation Bollinger Band. This plays off the previous idea that the trend has exhausted when the currency pair closes outside of the uptrend or downtrend zones. If it does not close out of the zone, then the trend remains intact.

In an uptrend, the way to find value is to wait for the currency pair to dip and retrace to the upper first standard deviation Bollinger Band. At that point, if we were looking to join the trend, we could go long with a stop placed slightly below the 15-day Simple Moving Average. Once again, a T1-T2 method of managing the trade should be used because we never know how much further the trend could go.

In a downtrend where a currency pair is falling like a rock, we would wait for it to rally back toward the lower first standard deviation Bollinger Band before joining the move. When it reaches that point, we could short with a stop placed slightly above 15-day moving average.

Exhibit 8.2 shows how Double Bollinger Bands can be used to find value within a trend. All of the entry points have been circled. Between June and July of 2010, the GBP/USD was in a very strong uptrend that took it from 1.46 to a high of 1.54. Within the uptrend there were eight opportunities to buy at value once the daily candle had closed, which is generally between 4 and 5 P.M. EST. If the currency pair closed outside of the band, the trade should not be taken. In all but one of those trades, the GBP/USD continued its prior trend. This is the type of hit ratio that we want to look for. No trading strategy will work 100 percent of the time, but we only want to trade strategies that yield far more profitable trades than unprofitable ones.

In the same GBP/USD chart, we can see that prior to movement between June and July, the GBP/USD was in a strong downtrend that brought it from 1.52 down to

Exhibit 8.2 Where's the Value in This Trend? A GBP/USD Daily Chart

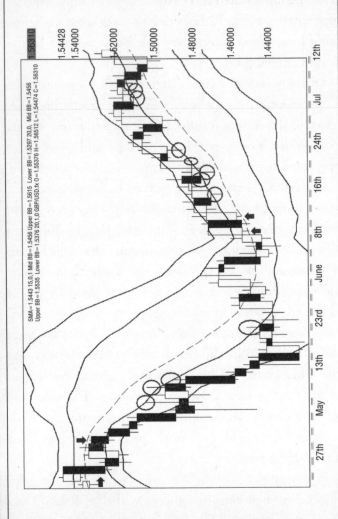

SMA=1.5443 15,0,1 Mid BB=1.5456 Upper BB=1.5615 Lower BB=1.5297 20,0, Mid BB=1.5456
Upper BB=1.5535 Lower BB=1.5376 20,1,0 GBP/USD.fx O=1.55376 H=1.55512 H=1.56512 L=1.54474 C=1.56310

Source: GFT Dealbook 360.

1.43. The move lasted less than a month but it was strong enough to have a big impact on the currency, and anyone caught long would have most likely been stopped out. In this downtrend, there were also a handful of opportunities to join the move at value. Exhibit 8.2 shows at least four opportunities on the short side. Selling at the first standard deviation Bollinger Band with a stop slightly above the 15-period moving average (the dotted line) would have given you a good value point to join the downtrend and yielded positive trades as long as you exited properly.

Now exiting the trade is of course the key. Sometimes buying or selling at the first band will provide the perfect entry that gets us into a multiple-day move that lasts for a few hundred pips. However, the more common scenario is that the currency pair will rebound that day and retrace the next, just as it did throughout the months of June and July. The general path of the GBP/USD was upward, but on the way there, the currency pair had both up and down days. This makes it extremely important to implement the T1-T2 method of exiting the trade. The first half of the position should be exited at a conservative pip profit of 30 to 60 pips, which may be less than the amount risked, but that is okay because the key to this methodology is to hit more winners than losers. Then once the profits have been locked in on the first half of the position, the stop on the rest of the position should be moved to the original entry price. If the currency pair continues to move in our favor, then we would adjust the stop accordingly. The trailing stop can be set at any amount that you are comfortable with—I personally like to use a trailing stop of 30 pips on the major currency pairs.

Getting into a New Trend

Finally, the Double Bollinger Bands can also be used to get into a new trend. We have talked about how a currency pair is in an uptrend when it trades between the two upper Bollinger Bands and in a downtrend when it trades between the two lower Bollinger Bands. Yet at some point it had to get into the bands first, and the point where it enters the uptrend or downtrend zones creates an opportunity to join a new trend that could be emerging. When the currency pair ends the NY session (4 P.M. Eastern Time) within the first and second bands, there is a reasonable chance that it will remain within the bands for days to come.

Take a look again at Exhibit 8.2. Starting from the left to the right of the chart, the first arrow points to a day when the GBP/USD has gone from the range-trading zone into the downtrend zone, and the next day, there was continuation. The continuation was not very significant because it only lasted for only 24 hours before the GBP/USD recovered. However, three days later, the same pattern occurs, where the GBP/USD once again closes within the downtrend zone, but in this case, it becomes a strong move that lasts for almost a month. The first example is the scenario that occurs more often, but the second scenario is not all that uncommon either. Therefore, it is extremely important to implement the T1-T2 methodology of exiting the trade because we never know if it will become a small move or a large one. We can hope that all of Double Bollinger Band trades will get us into a new trend that lasts for weeks, but we need to be realistic and recognize that the move may also last for only a few hours. Therefore, bag your winners quickly and let the market determine whether it wants to give you more profit.

The third arrow from the left in the chart shows another close into the Double Bollinger Bands, but in this case, it is into the uptrend zone. Unfortunately, this is a failed trade and I always like to show losing trades along with winning ones to remind everyone that no trading strategy will work 100 percent of the time. Finally, the fourth arrow from the left of the chart shows the GBP/USD once again closing into the uptrend zone; this time, it indeed marks the beginning of a prolonged uptrend that lasts for almost a month.

The Double Bollinger Bands are my favorite technical indicators and the secret ingredient to my forex trading. I hope they will help you in your trading as well.

Get It? Got It? Good!

- The Bollinger Band Method is great for finding trends. If a currency pair is trading between the upper or lower Double Bollinger Bands, then it is in trend!
- When a currency enters the up- or downtrend zone, it's a signal that a new trend could emerge.
- The trend might be exhausting if a currency pair moves outside of the Double Bollinger Bands.
- Who wants to pay up when they can wait for a bargain to come to them? Wait to enter a trend until the currency retraces to the inside Bollinger Bands.

Chapter Nine

So You're a Trader?

Fast and Furious for Quick Profits

SPEED SELLS. TAKE THE MOVIE *The Fast and the Furious*—surely one of those movies only speed demons could love. If you haven't seen the original film, which was released in 1954, or one of the many sequels, it is basically an over-the-top, testosterone-filled, adrenaline-pumping series about modified street cars that maneuver through daring stunts as part of the illegal underground world of street car racing. Although *The Fast and the Furious: Tokyo Drift* only brought in $60 million at the box office, the 2001, 2003, and 2009 versions of the movie raked in more than

$100 million each. Despite being panned by the critics, the franchise is a big success, proving that more than 10 million moviegoers love the series.

Another big hit in the world of entertainment is the Grand Theft Auto video game franchise. With 14 different titles based everywhere from Chinatown to the fictional state of San Andreas, it has sold over 120 million copies worldwide. These games are such a big hit that in 2009, the *Guinness Book of World Records* listed Grand Theft Auto as #3 on their list of Top 50 console games of all time, based upon impact and lasting legacy, outshined by only *Super Mario Kart* (#1) and *Tetris* (#2).

These movies and video games appeal to people who thrive on speed. However, even for those of us who find no pleasure in watching *The Fast and the Furious* or playing Grand Theft Auto, we may be more addicted to speed than we think. In a world where many people believe that time is money, faster is almost always better.

The desire for speed is even more common among traders. Most people don't have the time or mental capacity to sit in front of their computer screen, drink loads of coffee, and trade 24 hours a day, which is part of the reason they are attracted to short-term trading. However, it is not just time that separates those who seek out speed and those who avoid it. Some people just thrive on the adrenaline rush of watching the trade move rapidly in their favor, while others prefer to put on the trade with stops and limits, go out and play a game of golf, and let the trade work itself out. Although most people would say that they certainly prefer golfing to sitting in a dark room trading, in reality, some of us cannot peel ourselves away from the screen when we have a live trade.

Riding Momentum

The idea behind short-term or fast and furious trading is that we want to be in and out of the market quickly. One of the best ways of doing so is to ride momentum. Short-term trading is usually the most effective when the forex markets are active—generally during the European trading session (2 A.M. to 12 P.M. EST), which also covers the first half of the New York trading session. Currencies will also be particularly active immediately after economic data is released.

A number of different technical indicators and strategies can be used to identify a momentum move, but if we look beneath the hood, the moves are usually triggered by one of two things—the beginning of a trading session or economic data. The way currency traders behave at the market open can be difficult to predict, but the way they respond to economic data is not rocket science. If the economic data is extremely positive, there is a good chance that forex traders will drive up the value of the currency. If it is very weak, then there is a good chance that they will sell it aggressively.

At the end of the day, most short-term trend-following or momentum strategies will set up as a result of an economic release or a strong sentiment in the forex market, so it may be smart to just trade the event risk. Although looking for reversals or relief rallies are also tactics employed by short-term traders, the trending nature of currencies tends to favor continuation over reversals.

Sifting through the Headlines

Taking a trade based on a news release can be risky because the markets are exceptionally volatile after the release and brokers could widen their spreads. However, if we are fast and furious with managing the trade and stick with the major pairs (pairs dominated by the dollar), trading news releases can still be fruitful.

When trading the news, there are three questions that we need to ask ourselves before every trade: Is the news important? Is the surprise large enough? And is the surprise in line with the market's sentiment?

1. Is the news important? The first task at hand is to figure out what matters and what doesn't. Just because it rains today has no significance unless we have been in a drought for the past three months. In Chapter 5, we listed the top three pieces of potentially market-moving economic data for any country, which are the employment reports, retail sales, and manufacturing and service sector activity data, also known as the ISM or PMI reports. In addition to these, the Gross Domestic Product (GDP) releases and the inflation reports (consumer and producer prices) are also tradable. What is not tradable are reports like the Beige Book because there is no concrete number for comparison, data is released weekly, and any Japanese or Swiss economic reports are almost always overshadowed by the general sentiment in the market. If you are having a tough time figuring out if the data is tradable or not, most forex sites will list the impact that each piece of data may have on the currency. High-impact events are the ones that we want to trade.

2. Is the surprise large enough? The second question is the trickiest of the three because it is subject to interpretation, but the good thing is that the market will usually do the interpretation for you. As a rule of thumb, if the number is greater or less than the forecast by more than 5 percent, it is considered a big surprise, but sometimes a 2 percent surprise is enough to elicit a big reaction in the currency. So what should you do? Just wait and see how the market responds to the release. If the currency pair barely budges, then most likely, the surprise is not that significant. If the currency pair immediately shoots higher or falls like a rock, there is a good chance that the market was surprised. The key is to wait five minutes before getting into the trade to make sure that the currency responds the way that it is supposed to. In other words, a positive surprise should drive the currency pair higher and a negative surprise should drive it lower.

3. Is the surprise in line with the market's sentiment? The third question is important because sometimes the economic data is something that we would normally expect to elicit a big reaction, but for whatever reasons the rally fizzles quickly or traders simply don't care. This typically occurs when something else is overshadowing the data and driving the general sentiment in the forex market. It could be anything from the risk appetite to U.S. data or concerns about problems in Europe. If the economic data surprise or "fundamentals" is in line with the prevailing sentiment in the market, it is a stronger trade. In other words, if the market wants to buy dollars and retail sales are strong, it normally gives forex traders an even better reason to send the greenback higher. However, if the market is worried about the outlook of the U.S. economy because the Federal Reserve is warning that there will be more trouble to come, then good data may not do much for the dollar because it would be looked at with skepticism.

Quantifying a touchy-feely thing such as the prevailing sentiment in the market can be difficult, but moving averages can help because they measure the current trend in the market by averaging a certain number of past prices. If the data is good and the currency pair is trading above the 50-period moving average on a 5-minute chart (or the data causes the currency to break above the moving average), then there is a better chance that sentiment and fundamentals will support the trade. However, if the data is good and the currency pair is trading well below the 50-period moving average, then it suggests that the prevailing sentiment does not support the economic surprise. In this case, we will not take the trade because we want to have as many key variables aligned in our favor as possible.

To summarize, we only want to trade economic data that is important, with surprises that are large enough to trigger a reaction in the currency, and only if the economic data is in line with the general sentiment in the market. With these guidelines in hand, let me show you how fast and furious news trading works.

How Fast and Furious Trading Works

On July 15, 2010, U.S. producer prices were scheduled for release; before taking the trade, I asked myself the three questions introduced earlier.

Question 1 is whether the news release is important and PPI is a tradable economic release. Question 2 is whether the surprise is large enough—the forecast was for prices to fall by 0.1 percent and at 8:30 A.M. New York time, we learned that producer prices fell 0.5 percent, which was significantly worse than the market anticipated. Almost instantaneously, the U.S. dollar fell against the Japanese yen, and after the first 5 minutes of the release, the currency pair was trading well below the 50-period moving average on the 5-minute chart, providing the answer to the third question of whether sentiment is now in line with the economic release.

For most people, waiting five minutes before entering the trade can be extremely frustrating because they are eager to press the sell button and start participating. However, it's important to wait and let the initial volatility settle and to avoid immediate reversals. In the case of USD/JPY, once I had seen the 5-minute candle close sharply lower after the weaker economic report, it was time to enter into the trade.

Exhibit 9.1 shows the price action in USD/JPY when PPI was released and where I entered into the short trade, which was around 87.95. Since the surprise was significant enough and the prevailing sentiment in the market turned bearish dollars as a result of the release, the sell-off in USD/JPY had strong continuation. Over the next 90 minutes, USD/JPY fell from 87.95 to a low of 87.20, or 75 pips. At this point, you should ask *Where is the stop?* because every trade should have one. The best place to

Exhibit 9.1 A 5-Minute Chart Showing the USD/JPY Reaction to Producer Prices

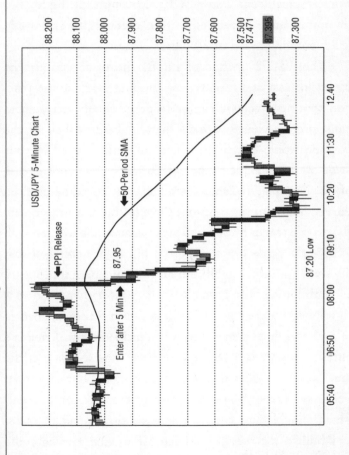

Source: GFT Dealbook 360.

put the stop on a short trade is the high of the data candle (in this case 88.26), but if that were too far away, then I would typically use a stop of 30 to 35 pips. If the high of the data candle is very close to the entry price, I would use a minimum stop of 20 pips.

The T1-T2 method of exiting the trade can also be useful for fast and furious news trading because the reaction to a news release can be large or small; you want to bank profits when you have them. The first half of the position would be closed when the trade moved in your favor by the amount risked, which was 31 pips in the case of our example, and then a trailing stop could be used on the remainder of the position. I like to trail the stops on my short-term trades by 20 to 30 pips because it is wide enough to give the trade breathing room but tight enough that it does not eat into a significant amount of floating profits.

Exhibit 9.2 is an example of why waiting five minutes is so important. On July 23, 2010, Canada was scheduled to release consumer prices. Like U.S. inflation data, Canada's inflation report is a tradable release. The forecast at the time was for prices to remain unchanged, but at 7 A.M. EST, we learned that consumer prices fell 0.1 percent, which should have been bearish for the Canadian dollar and bullish for the U.S. dollar. If we did not have the 5-minute rule, we would have gone long USD/CAD immediately, but by waiting five minutes, we can see that the

Exhibit 9.2 A 5-Minute Chart Showing the USD/CAD Reaction to Consumer Prices

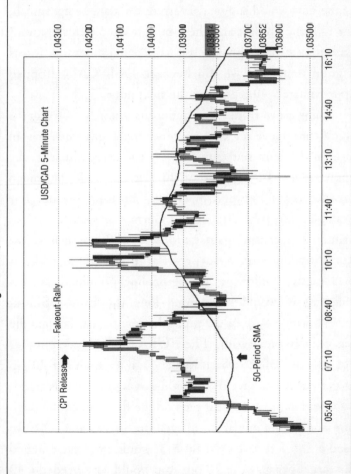

Source: GFT Dealbook 360.

market deems the data insignificant because the 5-minute candle in USD/CAD did not close in positive territory as the data would suggest. Despite the data being bullish, the rally did not last and the 5-minute candle closed lower, flashing a strong signal to tell us to avoid the trade. It was a good thing that we did because USD/CAD dropped approximately 40 pips over the next hour.

Some news trades are generous enough to trigger a significant move in the currency pair like the one in Exhibit 9.1, but that is not always the case, which is why applying the T1-T2 method to exit the trade can mean the difference between a winning or losing trade. For example, on July 20, 2010, German producer prices printed 0.6 percent against a forecast of 0.2 percent—data worth trading with a surprise large enough to make it meaningful. Following the guidelines outlined in this chapter, we would have gone long the EUR/USD at 1.2996 with a stop of 20 pips (the low of the data candle was only 16 pips away). The EUR/USD extended higher but only to 1.3028, which was enough to reach our 20 pip target but not to give us any additional pips. In this trade, we would have banked 20 pips on the first half of the position and gotten out at breakeven on the remainder. If we used a 2 to 1 risk/reward ratio, it would not have reached the target because the 20 pip stop would have needed a 40 pip profit target of 1.3036. The secret to fast and furious trading is to pick up as many of these smaller winners as possible while waiting for the economic surprises that trigger the big movers. Usually with news trading, the first target can be hit within the first hour.

Bear in mind, trading news events can be risky and there could be slippage that occurs when the orders are not filled at the exact price that they are set at because the markets are moving quickly. To minimize this risk, wait a few minutes after the news is released before taking any trade to allow volatility to settle.

Get It? Got It? Good!

- News moves markets.
- If the data is significant and the surprise is big enough, the move in the currency should continue.
- Filter out the noise and trade the data only if the sentiment in the market supports it.
- It pays to be patient. Wait five minutes before taking the trade to ensure that other traders will react to the number, too.
- Use the T1-T2 method to lock in winners by scaling out and managing the trade.

Chapter Ten

Risky Business

~

*Protecting Your Money in
Uncertain Times*

IF YOU WANT SOMETHING GOOD OUT OF LIFE, you're probably going to have to take a risk. Life (and trading) is just
plain risky business. So what's the difference between a
novice risk taker and a professional? It's all in the preparation. Let's say I've decided to climb Mount Everest—
with no training or previous experience, my expedition
would basically be a suicide mission.

At 29,002 feet, Mount Everest is the highest peak on
our planet and it attracts thousands of adventure seekers

every year. However, out of the 4,102 people who attempted to climb Mount Everest between 2008 and 2009, 216 did not survive. That's a 5 percent fatality rate for semi-professionals, but if the average person on the street were to attempt the climb, their potential fatality rate would be closer to 90 percent.

It is an understatement to say that conditions on the mountain are extreme. Most guide companies aren't willing to take their chances on the people who can't meet a strict set of guidelines. Alpine Ascents, one of the top guide companies, requires potential climbers to participate in a weeklong training course. In addition, they need to have climbed a series of other high-altitude mountains and prove they are in excellent physical condition (after all, they must be able to carry a 30-pound backpack for multiple days). Lastly, they must be mentally prepared to deal with strenuous situations at high altitudes.

The company only has one expedition per year in April or May, when the weather is the most cooperative. Why does Alpine Ascents have so many rules? Because they know that no matter how many times they have taken groups to the summit, it will still be risky.

Although you may not be planning an expedition up Mount Everest, being as prepared as possible and taking all the right precautions is something that everyone has experience with. For example, if you have children you will try to give them the best preparation for adult life that you possibly can. Some parents are so ambitious that certain preschools or kindergartens have waiting lists, requiring that you sign up your child before he or she is even born; usually these are the schools that charge steep tuition fees! Then as they get older, parents may send their kids to science camp, weekend prep classes, and tutoring sessions to help them with their homework. By the time they are ready to take the SATs for college admission, they will have taken a course from Kaplan or Princeton to get them prepared for the actual tests. After all, a good SAT score significantly improves their chances of getting into an Ivy League university. Getting into a good school is important because it can land them a good job and secure a good future. This is not to say that every child who goes to private kindergarten and takes Kaplan SAT prep classes will have a great career, or that those who don't will flounder, but as parents, we look to do the most that we can to give them their best chance of success.

Our children are far more important than trading or investing, but the reason Alpine Ascents takes such great precautions with their climbers and we do the same with our kids is that everyone wants to succeed and not fail. The same thought process needs to be applied to trading and investing because we want to succeed and not fail.

Therefore, we want to find trading opportunities that have low risk.

Sticking with High-Probability Trades

What professional traders look for are the "high-probability" trades, or the ones with the most variables aligned in their favor. Here are some secrets to determining whether a trade is high probability or not.

Let's say that the EUR/USD is in an uptrend and you see an opportunity to buy the currency pair on a retracement or dip. If you were trading purely on what you saw in a single chart or setup, you would most likely just dive right in and buy. Unfortunately, that is akin to driving down the road with blinders on! At minimum, it is important to take a look at the general trend in the market because being unaware of your environment can lead to unnecessary risks.

Fundamental and technical indicators as well as market sentiment are three factors that can affect every trade. If you can wait for those factors to line up in your favor, you have a far greater chance of reducing your risk and landing a potential profit. Ask yourself these questions to help decide whether a trade is worth the risk or not:

1. **How deep is the retracement or dip?** Imagine that you accidently cut your finger with a knife while chopping vegetables. The deeper the cut, the

longer it will take for your finger to heal. If it is just a shallow slice, then a band-aid will do the trick but if you accidently chopped off part of your finger, then it is far more complicated and a hospital visit would be necessary. In trading, a very strong retracement or dip is much more difficult to recover from than a shallow decline. Therefore, buying after a deep correction in an overall uptrend is generally a lower probability trade than buying after only a small retracement. Just as a deep cut increases the risk of losing a finger, a deep correction increases the risk of the currency pair breaking its uptrend.

2. **Is there a good fundamental reason behind the decline in the currency pair?** If the decline in the currency pair was triggered by a very disappointing economic data such as an abysmal report on consumer spending, then it is a lower probability trade that you may want to reconsider because short-term fundamentals are not on your side. However, if there is no major reason to explain the dip, then the coast is clear and there's a greater chance that the uptrend will resume.

3. **Could tomorrow's news release hurt the trade?** When trading the EUR/USD, it is also important to check to see if there is a piece of Eurozone or

U.S. economic data scheduled for release over the next 24 hours that could affect your trade. For example, if German retail sales are on the calendar and the market believes the data could be strong, it creates the backdrop for a higher probability trade. This would also be true if there is U.S. economic data on the calendar that the market expects to be weak. However, if there is reason to believe that the German data will surprise to the downside or U.S. data will surprise to the upside, then it may be better to pass on the trade.

4. **What is the general sentiment in the market? Does it support the trade?** Considering the general sentiment in the market, known as its "risk appetite," is also very important. For example, if the Dow plunged 300 points, there is a good chance that the Asian markets will trade lower in the next session because if American traders are nervous, there is a good chance that Asian traders will be as well. Therefore, it may not be such a good idea to buy the EUR/USD on a dip after a sharp sell-off in stocks because the dip could turn into further losses if Asian traders join in on the selling. However, if risk appetite is steady and equities ended up, flat, or only slightly lower, then the coast is clear. If the risk appetite is actually

positive with traders optimistic enough to rally stocks, then there is a greater chance that the rally in the EUR/USD will resume.

5. **Which key levels could affect the trade?** Key levels on a chart, or technical indicators, are also important. If the dip in the EUR/USD stopped just above a significant support level like 1.3000, assuming the support level continues to hold, going long EUR/USD would be a higher probability trade. However, if it broke below the support level, then there is scope for additional losses if support turns into resistance. In this case, it may be better to pass on the trade.

These five questions are guidelines that can be applied to both trading and investing but they are not rules that are set in stone. Oftentimes the answers to these questions will conflict and that is when our judgment should be used to determine which factors are more and less important.

If You're a Short-Term Trader . . .

For short-term traders, there are two additional points that can be considered to create even higher probability trades.

One year when I was at a traders' conference in Florida, I met a tall middle-aged trader named Dave, who said he was having a difficult time turning a profit in his forex trading. I asked him to tell me a little about his trading strategy. He responded by saying he likes to look for breakouts. I pressed for more details and he described his trading day.

Dave is married with two children and works as a full-time accountant during the day—a typical American lifestyle. He comes home from work, has dinner with his wife and kids, watches TV for about an hour, goes into his home office, turns on the computer, and begins trading. He starts by drawing trendlines on 5-minute charts to capture the range over the past few hours and then looks for breakouts. What is wrong with this picture?

The problem is that when Dave gets around to trading, it is approximately 8 P.M. East Coast time, which is the beginning of the Asian trading session. Unfortunately, this is the time when more "fake-outs" than breakouts occur because the beginning of the Asian session is typically one of the quietest times in the currency market. Most of the major currencies usually trade in very tight ranges between the end of the New York trading session (around 4 P.M. Eastern Time) and the beginning of the European trading session (around 2 A.M. Eastern Time). This means Dave is looking for breakouts at the worst time possible. Therefore, when it comes to short-term trading, two other points need to be considered:

1. **Is it the right time of day for my trading strategy?** It is important to realize that certain times of the day are more suitable to certain trading strategies. Very often currencies may fluctuate in a range before an important U.S. economic release, but the worst thing to do would be to try to pick short-term tops and bottoms at that time because of the high risk of a breakout. If a breakout or trend-following strategy sets up when the European and U.S. markets are both open, then it creates a higher probability trade because there are enough participants in the market to fuel continuation. If a breakout or trend-following opportunity presents itself at any other time, we need to be a bit more skeptical about the quality of the trade.

2. **Is this the best currency pair to trade?** Picking the right currency pair to trade can mean the difference between successful and unsuccessful trades. In fast and furious news trading (Chapter 9), we only traded the majors, but that may not always be the best option. For example, there are many cases where U.S. and Canadian economic data are released at the same time. If the Canadian data is very weak, one would assume that the best currency pair to buy after the news is released is USD/CAD. This is true if the U.S. economic data is

stronger than expected, but if it is weak, then the U.S. dollar and the Canadian dollar could both decline, leading to no major continuation in USD/CAD. In that case, it may be better to consider expressing the Canadian news trade through another currency pair such as AUD/CAD or CAD/JPY, which will be less affected by the U.S. economic data. The same is true if you have a good piece of European data but the market is bullish toward the dollar for one reason or another. Then perhaps buying euros against the pound is the higher probability trade.

These are judgment calls that short-term traders must make at the time of the trade, and they are important because they can mean the difference between a successful and an unsuccessful trade. It's worth the extra minute you'll take before diving into a trade.

The Key Is Yours

You can never be 100 percent certain about whether a trade will be successful or not, but you can increase the probability of it being successful by looking for only high-quality trades. This extra effort is important if you value your hard-earned money (and I think you should!). I am a big believer in high-probability trading and the questions in this chapter are the ones that I ask myself before every single trade.

The point is to have as many stars aligned in your favor as possible on your trades and not to expose it to unnecessary and amateur risks. Trading will always be risky business, but making sure the fundamentals, technicals, and market sentiment support your trade every time will give you the highest probability of success. The keys to successful trading are to have an edge, minimize the risks, and not be greedy!

Get It? Got It? Good!

- Shallow retracements are a sign of higher probability trades.
- A trend is more likely to continue if there is no fundamental reason for the dip.
- Seek out trades that are supported by upcoming economic data.
- Trades that are in line with the general sentiment in the market are a better choice.
- Make sure key levels will not stall the trade.
- Short-term traders should know what time of day is suitable for their trading strategy and to pick the right currency pairs.

Chapter Eleven

The Top 10 Mistakes

—— ∼ ——

. . . *So You Don't Make Them*

In 2009, George Clooney starred in the Oscar-nominated film *Up in the Air*, a story about a corporate executioner who spends 322 days out of the year on the road. His character, Ryan Bingham, is an efficiency expert who knows all the shortcuts to get through security checkpoints swiftly so he can spend the shortest amount of time waiting for his plane. I may not fly nearly as much as Bingham, but when I do, I like to test cutoff times and arrive at the airport minutes before my flight boards.

My tendency to wait until the 11th hour before arriving at the airport drives my coworkers, friends, and family nuts. Most people I know get to the airport one and a half hours before a domestic flight and three hours before an international flight. Yes, these are the Transportation Security Administration's recommendations, but they are designed for the casual traveler and not the Ryan Binghams of the world. Like Bingham, I always check in online, print out my boarding pass, make sure there are no liquids, aerosols, or gels in my carry-on luggage, and know that my frequent flier elite status allows me to bypass long security lines. For domestic flights, I usually arrive at the airport no more than 45 minutes before boarding and for international flights no more than 90 minutes. Have I ever missed a flight? Only once when I was headed to Italy for vacation. Did I learn from my mistake? Nope, because in the 10 years and hundreds of flights since then, I have never missed another flight—and it was not because I started to arrive at the airport earlier. Should most people do as I do? Probably not. The main reason I wait until the last minute to head to the airport is that I can squeeze in a few extra hours of sleep or an extra hour of work, and the worst that can happen is I will get bumped onto the next flight. I factor in the worst-case scenario before every flight and know that it can be handled with a phone call and some patience.

However, not everyone can afford to miss their flight because of connections or appointments. The same goes for trading not everyone can afford to make a ton of mistakes. Part of trading is about managing the trade and part of it is about managing ourselves. We all have our own level of risk tolerance, but having met thousands of successful and unsuccessful forex traders, I can tell you that most forex traders make the same mistakes. In general, human emotions can kill profits. Some traders become so frustrated that they decide to codify their trading rules, which basically lets the computer do all of the work and eliminates human intervention. However, computers can't adjust to changing market environments.

Most of the mistakes that traders make are not new; for those people who are able to avoid them from the very beginning, the path to successful trading will be smoother. Whether you're new to forex trading or have made some mistakes already, review this list of Top 10 Mistakes of Forex Traders and hopefully, it will save you a lot of time and money.

Mistake #1: Trading Out of Boredom or Anger.   The trader's high never goes away. Regardless of whether you have been trading for a month, a year, or a decade, there is always an initial adrenaline rush when you put on the trade. However, being bored and seeking excitement is one of the worst reasons to trade. When the markets are quiet and you are looking to put on a position, there is a very good chance that after scanning through a few charts over a few different time frames that you will convince yourself that the trade is right. Unfortunately, what you are actually doing is forcing a trade, which can eventually lead to losses. Professional traders wait for a currency pair to set up according to their plan and do not create a plan based upon the desire to trade.

Being angry is even worse than being bored. Have you ever heard the saying that revenge is never sweet? The most dangerous time for any trader occurs right after a major loss. The instinct for revenge trading (the desire to get it all back at once) can be far more damaging than the initial loss, leading many traders to make impulsive, irrational decisions that often lead to complete destruction of the account. It is much better to chip away at the losses by assuming less and less risk until the losses are recovered. This strategy stands in sharp contrast to what many novice traders do, which is to create even more risk by trying to revenge trade after a big loss.

Mistake #2: Having Unrealistic Expectations. I will never forget the time that I encountered an overly eager trader at a forex expo who asked me if my trading returns were better than those of the winners of forex trading contests. I responded by saying, "Considering that the winners make between 500 and 3,000 percent return in one month, which would equate to a yearly return of 6,000 to 360,000 percent, there is a very good chance that he is taking a lot of risk, trading irrationally, using a strategy that he would never use if he were trading a significant amount of real money." Usually these contests are either for demo trading accounts: minis and micros where the average account size is between $500 and $2,500. Even the best hedge fund managers in the world are not able to make 1,000 percent return, let alone 360,000 percent return on a consistent basis. Having unrealistic expectations encourages greater risk taking, which is one of the primary reasons many new traders blow up their accounts. Seasoned forex traders are happy if they can beat the performance of the S&P 500 and elated if they can consistently generate double-digit returns every year. The key to being a successful forex trader is to approach it like any other asset class and to expect reasonable and not sky-high returns.

Mistake #3: Taking Highly Correlated Trades. What many new traders fail to realize is that currencies will often move in the same direction. For example, on any given day, if the Australian dollar is up against the U.S. dollar, there is a very good chance that the New Zealand dollar appreciated as well. Many new forex traders will look at their charts and see that the AUD/USD and NZD/USD are breaking out at the same time and will naively go long both currencies. However, by doing so, the trader is basically doubling up on the same position. This redundant exposure could be intentional, but for most new traders it probably isn't, which can be a big mistake because if one comes crashing down, there is a good chance the other will follow. The reason currencies will move in the same direction is the U.S. dollar. On most days, the U.S. dollar will be either up against all of the major currencies or down. The magnitude of the moves will be different, which may be a reason that a trader has decided to spread his risk between the AUD/USD and NZD/USD, but if that is not the intention, then rather than being diversified, the exposure is highly concentrated, which creates a hidden risk in the positions.

Mistake #4: Failing to Use a Stop.   Another question that is asked often at trade shows is the importance of using a stop. I am always shocked to find out that many forex traders do not believe in using stops. Their argument is that if they do not use a stop, the currency will eventually get back to their initial entry. This is true until it isn't. When the trend in currencies is strong, it can move aggressively in one direction with little retracement. Eventually, it *may* get back to prior levels, but that could takes days, weeks, months, and sometimes even years. Unfortunately, markets can stay irrational far longer than most people can stay solvent, which means there may not be enough equity in the account to last until the currency pair finally gets back to its prior level. It goes without saying that all traders should use a stop. Trading at its core is ultimately an exercise in controlling the chaotic and often unpredictable markets. If you do not use a stop, you are at the mercy of the market and lose all control of your trade. At that time, the best thing to think about is whether the trade would still be attractive if you were not already in the position.

Mistake #5: Taking Unnecessary Risks.   New Yorkers are notoriously guilty of jaywalking. Even 80-year-old grandmothers will avoid walking to the end of the street and waiting for the light to change before crossing. However, every time that I have seen an older person jaywalk it is over the weekend and in the early morning when most of the city is still sleeping. With decades of life experience, grandmothers and grandfathers know that it is far less risky to jaywalk at a time when the city is deserted in an area that is relatively quiet than during rush hour in Times Square. In fact, they would probably never jaywalk at that time and in that madness because it is an unnecessary risk. When it comes to trading, holding a position over the weekend when the finance ministers and central bankers are holding a summit is an example of taking an unnecessary risk. The outcome of these meetings is oftentimes unpredictable and can trigger a gap open on Sunday evening. Staying on top of upcoming news releases and events can help new traders avoid exposing the position to unnecessary risks.

Mistake #6: Being Too Patient with Losers and Not Patient Enough with Winners.   Inexperienced traders are usually too patient with their losers and not patient enough with their winners. Cut your losses quickly and let your winners ride is a common piece of advice that traders will receive. However, is it even more relevant to forex trading because of how strong trends can be. Many traders fall victim to the mistake of nursing their losers until they become so large that it wipes out their account. Some will even keep their losing trade open and trade around the losses hoping to recover at least some of it back. Yet these are most likely the same traders who will abandon their trades as soon as it turns a small profit. Unfortunately, this is not the most efficient way to trade currencies. It is generally smarter to bag a small profit early and leave open a part of the position in case a large trend emerges.

Mistake #7: Being a "Possum Trader."   If you have ever had a losing trade and decided to shut off your computer or walk away with the hope that it will turn around if you stopped watching it, then you have fallen victim to what my good friend Rob Booker calls Possum Trading. You leave the position open, close your eyes, cross your fingers, and hope that the trade will work itself out.

Unfortunately, this almost never happens, and more often than not, the losses become even greater. Trading is a game of survival and closing your eyes hoping that the fire will put itself out is not the right decision. If it is a small fire, it is smarter to put it out before it even comes close to burning down your house; if it is a large one, it is better to abandon your home and call in the firefighters. In trading, if the reason for the trade is no longer valid, then get out before the losses grow. Don't keep the trade on and turn into a possum.

Mistake #8: Taking on Too Much Leverage.   In 2008 when I traveled to Dubai for the very first time and we were driving down Sheikh Zayed Road, which is the equivalent of Las Vegas Boulevard, I could not help but notice the glamorous buildings and the numerous construction projects in process. It felt like half of the world's cranes were in a five mile radius. Gulf News puts it at closer to 20 percent at the time, which is still tremendous. Yet, considering that at one point the number of construction workers rivaled the number of Dubai citizens, it was clear that property developers were over-leveraged and a bubble was forming. When the bubble became too large, as it did in the United States, it burst, causing prices to fall 60 percent from their peak. The subprime turned financial crisis was a tough lesson in over-leveraging. Forex brokers will entice individual traders with very generous amounts of leverage, but risking anything greater than 5 to 10 percent of your account on any one trade is financial suicide. Leverage is a wonderful drug when the trade moves in your direction, but it is pure poison when the market is aligned against you.

Mistake #9: Over-Optimizing Your Strategy. Trading robots have become very popular over the past few years, and savvier traders have even learned to code their own trading strategies and create mini algos. However, the biggest mistake that these traders make is over-optimizing their strategy. What may work perfectly in one market environment will not work so well in others. Having spent a great deal of time creating systematic trading products, I have learned that most robots or algos work in either trend or range but rarely in both. So if someone is showing you backtested results with 1,000 percent returns, you should be highly skeptical because they have probably over-optimized their robot to show you a perfect trading record that will be difficult to replicate in reality. Markets are dynamic and their drivers change with time; therefore, it is important to use the appropriate strategies in the right trading environments. For example, applying trend-following or breakout trading strategies in quiet range-bound environments will usually lead to more losers than winners.

Mistake #10: Becoming a Demo Billionaire. Finally, don't become a demo billionaire. Nothing can replace live trading. According to my business partner, who loves to play video games with his son, trading a demo is like playing Halo 3 and thinking that you are ready for war. The moment you hear a shell explode near you in real life, you'd pee your pants. Just because you can make 500 percent return in your demo doesn't mean that you will be able to do the same in a live account. Once you start to see losses of $1,000 or $5,000, nervousness will cause you to question whether you should remain in the trade. One of the unique advantages of the forex market is that brokers provide new traders with different sized accounts, which allows them to ease into live trading. After making consistent profits on the demo, open up a mini trading account with a small amount of throwaway money. Make sure you can handle the psychological element of trading real money before you commit greater amounts of capital.

Regardless of your risk tolerance, or whether you arrive at the airport an hour or three hours in advance of a flight, nobody likes to make a mistake. Reviewing this list of the Top 10 Mistakes might save you from making one. Just make sure that you have a good reason for getting in and out of each trade and don't get emotional!

Chapter Twelve

Greetings from Nigeria, Please Help!

~

Detecting and Avoiding Forex Scams

ABOUT ONCE A WEEK I RECEIVE AN E-MAIL THAT begins like this:

Dear Sir,

I have been requested by the Nigerian National Petroleum Company to contact you for assistance in resolving a matter. The Nigerian National Petroleum Company has recently *concluded a large number of contracts for oil exploration in the sub-Sahara region. The contracts have immediately produced moneys equaling US$40,000,000.*

Your assistance is requested as a non-Nigerian citizen to assist the Nigerian National Petroleum Company, and also the Central Bank of Nigeria, in moving these funds out of Nigeria. If the funds can be transferred to your name, in your United States account, then you can forward the funds as directed by the Nigerian National Petroleum Company. In exchange for your accommodating services, the Nigerian National Petroleum Company would agree to allow you to retain 10%, or US$4 million of this amount.

However, to be a legitimate transferee of these moneys according to Nigerian law, you must presently be a depositor of at least US$50,000 in a Nigerian bank which is regulated by the Central Bank of Nigeria.

Sound familiar? Many people have heard of this infamous Nigerian e-mail scam and if you are like me, by the time I read the words "requested by the Nigerian . . . ," I have already hit the delete button. Depositing $50,000 for an immediate access to $40 million with a promise to return $36 million is too good to be true. Yet believe or not, thousands of Americans fall victim to this scam. A quick search on the Internet will reveal hundreds of stories of real Americans who for one reason or another have taken the bait. The reason most of us don't give these e-mails even a passing thought is because we know that when something sounds too good to be true, it probably is.

Scammers exist everywhere, including the financial market. Investing and trading is not easy because it takes hard work, discipline, and commitment. Some people are able to succeed relatively quickly but most struggle at first, which is why shortcuts are attractive. Traders are presented with a great many get-rich-quick offers, such as software that generates guaranteed profits for only $20 a month. These opportunities are enticing but never live up to their promises. The scams are always the same, only packaged in different ways. If anyone promises guaranteed profits, there is a 99.9 percent chance that it is a scam. There is no such thing as a money-making system that will generate guaranteed profits, and if it does exist, the person will be much more interested in managing millions and billions of dollars on the system than selling it to you for $20 a month. This type of scam exists in the equity and futures market so it should not be a surprise that it exists in forex as well. The key to avoiding a scam is to be smart and use common sense.

Avoiding popular forex mistakes is useful but avoiding scammers is even more important because you are giving up full control with very little transparency—someone can cheat you out of your money and you may not even know why. Scammers in the financial market typically reach their potential audience by e-mail, online advertisements, magazines, newspapers, or radio promotions. New scams pop up all the time, but they are rarely original and they usually fall into one of several categories. Some scammers offer to provide trading signals, a new system, or fund management and brokerage services. Whatever the scam, the message always boils down to one single idea, which is an offer to make a quick and easy buck.

The Signal Provider Scam

Signal providers are basically "experts" who sell trading recommendations with specific entry and exit levels. The types of people who subscribe to signals are usually people who are looking for someone to hold their hand while they learn how to trade or are looking for more trade ideas. Signal providers will send their trading recommendations to their subscribers via e-mail or text message and tell them exactly which currency to trade, when to buy or sell, how to exit, and where to place their stop. Essentially they spoon-feed the information to their clients, who will then either follow it wholeheartedly or compare it to their own analysis. As in any business, there are both honest and dishonest providers. Some signal providers are legitimate and actually care about sending quality trades to their subscribers, but others may not have such high scruples.

It is not always easy to tell if the signal provider is honest, but there are warning signs to watch for, including promises of 100 percent guaranteed forex winning signals or offers to make $1,000 per week (both of which are promotions that can be found by doing a quick online search for "forex signals"). Also beware of any offshore signal providers because, most likely, they have incorporated offshore to avoid taxes, lawsuits, or regulations that are required by countries that may have stricter rules to protect their consumers. If the results are audited and tracked on a live account, then there is a better chance that the signal provider is honest.

The Trading System Scam

Forex signal providers have been around for a very long time but in recent years the number of forex trading systems has exploded. They may also be called robots, expert advisers, or algos, but the concept is the same—they are computer programs that automatically execute trades based upon set parameters. The benefit of automated systems is that it removes fear and greed, which are the common human emotions that hold traders back. These systems are enticing because you don't need to watch for trades 24 hours a day, as the computer will do it for you. However, the biggest problem with using a trading system is the lack of transparency. When you are the developer of the system, you understand exactly how it works inside and out. When it is someone else's system that you have bought, most of the time you have no clue how it works. Trading systems are mostly trend following or range trading but rarely both. Finding a trading system that works well in both environments is like finding the holy grail of trading, and as a smart person once told me, if you have found the Holy Grail, why on earth would you share it?

For example, a forex trading system that only bought carry trades would have worked extremely well between 2001 and 2007. If the forex trading system provider only showed results from those years, the returns would have been extremely attractive. However, carry trades came crashing down in 2008, leading to significant losses. Forex robots tend to show results of idealized scenarios that are rarely sustainable over time. If the system creator is truly dishonest, they may have even over-optimized their results, showing only the perfect scenarios.

Promises of automated trading systems (also known as trading robots and expert advisors) that make claims of no losses 100 percent of the time is an obvious red flag, but the price of the automated system, robot, or expert advisors can also give you a hint of whether it is legitimate. If the trading system is really as great as they tout, then any smart developer would not be willing to offer it for free or even for a small one-time fee of $100. Beware of robots or expert advisers with results that are based only on demo accounts and not live accounts, trading systems with results for less than a year, and providers with no contact information. The robots are oftentimes repackaged and sold over and over again and under different names. Another scam is to sell indicators that repaint the past. Most technical indicators are fixed once a candle or bar has closed, but repainting indicators redraws the past data as new data comes in, which basically distorts the results and makes them far more attractive than what could be achieved in real time.

Managed Accounts or Managed Funds Scams

Managed accounts or managed funds are popular among investors who are interested in getting some exposure to currencies but do not have the time or knowledge to actually trade or invest their own money actively. Therefore, they seek the assistance of an expert who will manage their money for them. Investment funds that tout returns of 300 percent a month are clearly red flags. If you are evaluating a managed account, it is important to look for ones where the returns are realistic because it usually means they are maintaining some degree of discipline and risk control. Make sure that they do not use too much leverage and their drawdowns are tolerable. Managed funds that are run by professional money managers who are registered Commodity Trading Advisors or Commodity Pool Operators (or the equivalent in other countries) also tend to be more legitimate. Usually regulators who keep an eye on these registered parties will regularly review their marketing practices as well as their results to make sure they are factually accurate.

Like forex signal providers and trading systems, you should avoid the managers who are incorporated in suspicious countries and the ones who promise outrageous returns. It is also generally safer when your funds are held with a regulated broker rather than directly with the money manager.

More Scammers . . . Bucket Shop Brokers or Referring Parties

Believe it or not, forex brokers can also be scam artists. The National Futures Association regulates the retail foreign exchange industry in the United States and they have cited a number of brokers, large and small, for infractions. These include things such as misleading documentation or dealing practices. When picking a broker, make sure it is regulated in a country with strict guidelines such as the United States, United Kingdom, Japan, or Australia. The more countries that they are regulated in, the better. If your broker is domiciled in the Caribbean or anywhere else, that can be suspicious; it may be better to choose another broker because you may have less legal recourse when sending your money to an offshore broker than an onshore one.

If the broker is regulated in the United States, check the National Futures Association's web site (www.nfa .futures.org) to see if they have any infractions; then check the Commodity Futures Trading Commission's (CFTC) web site (www.cftc.gov) to see how well they are capitalized. In order to operate in the United States, retail foreign exchange brokers must have minimum net capital of $20 million with an additional volume-based minimum capital threshold that they must maintain. The U.S. regulator implemented this rule in 2009 (it was first introduced in 2007) to weed out the weakly capitalized brokers. The more capital that your broker has, the better because you never want to be in a situation where your accounts are frozen because your broker suddenly fell into bankruptcy after faulty position taking. We can never avoid this risk completely, but we can minimize it by trading with a well-capitalized broker. As of May 2010, the four largest retail forex brokers in the United States have adjusted net capital in excess of $75 million. Take a look and see how your broker compares.

It is also important to check the public forums and review sites to see if other customers have complained about the brokers that you are considering. All foreign exchange brokers will have problems with execution, slippage, requotes, or the stability of their platform at some point or another, but the ones who have these problems consistently should be avoided. There are thousands of forex brokers around the world and only a handful of regulated firms—those are the ones that you want to trade with.

10 TIPS FOR AVOIDING A FOREX SCAM

1. Stay away from opportunities that sound too good to be true.

2. Avoid any company that predicts or guarantees large profits.

3. Stay away from companies that promise little or no financial risk.

4. Don't trade on margin unless you understand what it means.

5. Question firms that claim to trade in the "Interbank Market."

6. Be wary of sending or transferring cash on the Internet, by mail, or otherwise.

7. Currency scams often target members of ethnic minorities via ethnic newspapers and television infomercials.

8. Be sure you get the company's performance track record.

9. Don't deal with anyone who won't give you their background.

10. Be alert to the warning signs of commodity "come-ons."

Source: CFTC, www.cftc.gov/ConsumerProtection/ FraudAwarenessPrevention/CFTCFraudAdvisories/fraudadv_forex .html.

Trust No One but Yourself

The best way to avoid scammers is to trust no one but yourself. If you are serious about being successful at currency trading, there is no need to rush because the market will still be waiting for you three months from now. Take your time to learn how the market works, learn the basics of how to read charts and use technical indicators, understand the fundamental drivers of currencies and how to manage your trades. Then do some due diligence on regulated retail foreign exchange brokers, open up demo accounts with a few of them, download their software, pick up the phone and have their staff walk you through their trading stations. Practice makes perfect so the next step is to practice trading on a demo account. Once you feel comfortable and have made money on the demo, deposit a small amount of money into a mini or micro account, practice some more and only after turning a consistent profit on a small amount of money should you start trading for real. Shortcuts may be enticing but nothing can replace a true understanding of how the market works. Don't waste money on the scammers, invest in educating yourself instead.

Whether it's a forex scam or a legitimate offer, use common sense and remember that there is no free lunch and fortunes aren't made overnight. If it sounds too good to be true, then it probably is.

Get It? Got It? Good!

- Avoid any company that predicts or guarantees large profits with little or no financial risk.
- Be wary of high-pressure tactics to convince you to send or transfer cash immediately to the firm, via overnight delivery companies, the internet, by mail, or otherwise.
- Be skeptical about unsolicited phone calls about investments from offshore salespersons or companies.
- If you have any questions, contact the Commodity Futures Trading Commission (CFTC).

Chapter Thirteen

Getting Down to Business

The Importance of a Good Trading Plan

NOW THAT YOU ARE ARMED WITH TRADING STRATEGIES, tips on avoiding the biggest mistakes made by forex traders, and the know-how to spot the scams, it is time to start trading—but before pressing the buy or sell buttons, you're going to need a plan.

In the 1980s, there was a very popular game show in the United States called *Press Your Luck*. The rules of the game were simple: Answer trivia questions to earn spins and then use the spins to win either cash or prizes on the 18-space game board. However, within the game board were a number of Whammies that, if landed on, would trigger a cute but deadly animation of a Tasmanian Devil–like character that would run across the screen and steal all of the contestant's money. As you can imagine, no contestants wanted their spin to land on a Whammy and so they chanted "No Whammy, No Whammy" as the board spun around. Yet as luck would have it, most people either had their money stolen by the Whammy or cashed out with less than $20,000. However, in 1984, a man named Michael Larson surprised everyone, including CBS, the network that carried the show, by winning $110,237 in cash and prizes, making him the biggest game show winner of his time.

Larson did not win because he rubbed a rabbit's foot for good luck. Prior to appearing on the game show, he had a clearly thought out and well-practiced plan of action. He spent six months studying the movement of the light used for the Big Board and *learned* how to consistently hit the squares containing bonuses and to never let the spinner stop on a Whammy. He recorded every episode of the game and spent hours each night watching the videos, freezing it frame by frame to look for patterns. Although some people may consider this cheating, Larson did not break any rules and the producers of the game show could not do anything but let him walk away with the winnings.

What separated Larson from other contestants was that he went on the game show armed with a plan that he spent months fine-tuning and practiced over and over again. Having this type of preparation and discipline would benefit all traders. Larson knew that he had only one opportunity to appear on the game show and therefore he needed to be as prepared as possible. However, unlike a game show contestant, you have the opportunity to trade every day.

Trading Is Not Your Hobby

In life, what separates professionals from novices is that professionals are always prepared. They do more homework than necessary just in case the unexpected occurs. A trading plan is the equivalent of any other professional's business plan. Smart traders know that they are more rational when evaluating a trade setup and less rational once the trade is unfolding. Acting on emotions once a trade is live can kill profits.

With a trading plan, it is much easier to stick to your original idea and not let a 10-pip move against the trade sway your conviction. In any business, there will undoubt-edly be setbacks, but as long as we trust our business model and, in this case, our trading strategy, you won't be discouraged when the trade moves slightly in the wrong direction. For anyone serious about making money trad-ing forex, it is important to approach it like a business and not a recreational hobby.

Start the Day Fresh

Starting the day by catching up on the news and checking your charts is a solid start to establishing a trading plan and one I recommend to any trader or investor.

The first thing to do every morning is to catch up on news flow. If you are obsessed with efficiency like I am, turn on CNBC or Bloomberg while getting ready in the morning to hear the top stories in the financial markets to make sure nothing crazy happened overnight. If you com-mute to work, pick up either the *Wall Street Journal* or the *Financial Times* on the way for a broader and deeper cov-erage on the themes in the market. When I get to the office, the first thing that I do after I turn on my com-puter is look at the economic data released overnight and scan the headlines for stories relating to currencies. Then I look at how Asian and European equities performed, as well as how U.S. equity futures are trading. All of this happens before I look at the charts because I want to get a clear picture of the data and the stories in the financial markets without having my judgment distorted by price action.

After catching up on news flow, it is time to check the quotes. I set up my quote screen in such a way that I can see exactly how the market is behaving at a glance. At the very top of my quote screen are the three U.S. equity indices followed by real-time quotes for the 21 most actively traded currency pairs. I organize my quote screen by the majors, then EUR/GBP, EUR/CHF, and the Japanese yen crosses (crosses are currency pairs that do not include the U.S. dollar). The more obscurely traded crosses, which are the currency pairs that do not include the dollar, are listed last. The reason I choose to organize it this way is that, at a quick glance, I can tell if all of the yen crosses are up or down for the day and whether the dollar has risen or fallen against all other major currencies. In addition to the latest quotes, I have columns for the high, low, the pip, and percentage change for the day. The percentage change also helps me quickly tell which currency is the best and worst performing.

Each of the quotes is linked to a real-time chart; after checking the quotes, I will scan through the charts to see if the overnight moves have caused the currency pairs to break any significant levels. Throughout the day I will be watching my quote screen to see how stocks and currencies are moving while periodically flipping through my charts.

Ready, Set, Plan!

After all of this pre-trade work, then it is time to plan my trades! Every trader should have a trading plan for short-term trades and another for long-term trades. Since I trade event risk, my short-term trade plan will be a bit different from my longer term position trade plan, which may key off indicators such as the Double Bollinger Bands.

For my short-term intraday trades, I like to ride the momentum off news releases as we discussed in Chapter 9. In order to maintain the utmost efficiency, I spend time in the evenings listing the events that I plan to trade the next day. Since I trade during the New York session, I usually trade U.S. and Canadian economic reports that are released at 8:30 A.M. Eastern Time or 10:00 A.M. data. Occasionally I have the opportunity to trade 7:00 A.M. Canadian employment data or the Australian and New Zealand economic reports that are released toward the end of my day. Regardless of whether I take these trades, I create my trading plan the previous day, listing the currency that I plan to trade. Sometimes I also have an opinion on how the data could surprise and open a small position 20 minutes before the number is released and add to it once the data is out.

Here's a sample of my initial Daily Trading Plan (read on and you will see how it changes):

Economic Data to Trade

U.S. Trade Balance @ 8:30 A.M.

   Confidence: HIGH

   Bearish USD (because of decline in ISM)

CAD Trade Balance @ 8:30 A.M.

   Confidence: MEDIUM

   Bearish CAD (because of decline in IVEY)

Australian Employment @ 9:30 P.M.

   Confidence: HIGH

Bullish AUD (employment component of PMIs increased)

I also trade a few other short-term strategies that are a bit more complex and explained in further detail in my book for intermediate traders titled *Day Trading and Swing Trading the Currency Market*. One of my favorites is called the Momo, which is another momentum-based strategy. So the next thing that I do is list the currency pairs that could be setting up for the Momo and the levels to watch.

Momo Setup in the Works

EUR/USD: on break above 1.3245

GBP/USD: on break above 1.5825

USD/JPY: on break below 88.20

I am up early so all of this preparatory work is done before 8 A.M. Eastern Time!

On this particular day, I am looking to short USD/JPY at 8:10 A.M. Eastern Time if the currency pair is trading below the 50-period SMA on the 5-minute chart at that time and only add to the position if the U.S. trade balance is weak. If it is strong, I would close out my USD/JPY short trade immediately and move into a new long USD/JPY trade five minutes after the release if the move takes the currency pair above the 50-period SMA as explained in Chapter 9. At the same time, I would be looking to buy or sell USD/CAD in the direction of the data and I will not forget to place a stop on the entire position and a first target (T1) on half of the position. Then I will leave the news trades alone and check back only if they are stopped out or the first target is reached.

Meanwhile, I have one eye on the EUR/USD and GBP/USD quotes to look for a Momo trade. If I have a USD/JPY news trade on, I will most likely not trade USD/JPY using a different strategy because it just creates confusion. Usually my news trades are closed out within the first few hours of trading. Since the Momo strategy is based on technical indicators, I will check the charts throughout the day to see if the levels that I listed above need to be changed or if other currency pairs and levels should be added to the list. By 1 P.M. to 2 P.M. Eastern Time, most of my shorter term trading is done.

At 4:30 P.M. Eastern Time, I will be looking for opportunities to join an existing trend or a new trend using the Double Bollinger Bands discussed in Chapter 8. First I will list the three types of setups and the possible opportunities that I am looking for in the following format:

Double Bollinger Band Retrace Opportunity

EUR/USD: Uptrend

GBP/USD: Uptrend

USD/JPY: Downtrend

Double Bollinger Band New Trend Opportunity

AUD/USD: Uptrend

Double Bollinger Band Reversal Opportunity

None

Then, applying the techniques discussed in Chapter 10, I look for the highest probability trades. Those are the ones that are supported by fundamentals, technicals, and market sentiment. To be more specific, if USD/JPY is in an uptrend and has retraced to the first standard deviation Bollinger Band, I will only buy the currency pair hoping for a continuation if the U.S. stock market ended the day marginally lower, flat, or higher, which means sentiment does not hurt my trade and if there is a piece of U.S. economic data tomorrow that I think will either be positive or neutral for the trade. If stocks fell significantly or if I have a strong reason to believe the next day's U.S. economic data will be dollar negative, I will most likely pass on the trade.

The Bollinger Band trades are usually held overnight so I will put in my stop along with a first target on half of the position. I will also put a second target for the remainder of the position that is much further away from the first target but still achievable in case there are big moves overnight when I am sleeping. Remember, be smart by considering the exit for the trade early on; it's just as important as finding a good point of entry.

When this is done, I list the economic data due for release tomorrow so I am prepared for the new trading day.

However, there is still one more trade to take on this particular day, which is a short-term trade on the heels of the Australian employment report. There is tradable

Australian or New Zealand economic data only once or twice a week so normally I can still go the gym and get a good night's rest before the whole process begins again.

Trading plans are different and evolve with time but are useful to develop a consistent regimen. In fact, all traders should strive to have a military-like discipline with the acumen to know when to take a trade and when to pass on it.

Know Your Loss Limit

In addition to a trading plan, it is also important to have a contingency plan. All good business owners are passively aware of their loss limit, which is the maximum amount that they are able and willing to lose if their business goes sour. For traders, this means knowing when to stop trading. Sometimes we will have a streak of bad luck that leads to a string a losers, and after a certain point, it may be better to just turn off the screen, walk away from the computer, and take a break from trading for a few days before starting again. A series of losers can lead to irrational trading behaviors that will inevitably lead to greater losses. As John Paulson once said, one of the key investments rules that he lives by is to "watch the downside, the upside will take care of itself."

To become a professional trader, it is important to develop a consistent regimen and to have a trading plan. Not only does it save time and get you into the mind-set of trading but it also reduces the potential impact of emotions. When you question your trade—and you inevitably will—the trading plan is there to remind you why you took the trade in the first place. If those reasons have changed, then closing the trade may be a good idea, but if they have not, then stick with it! In my case, I know exactly what I could potentially trade when I step into the office. This saves me time and allows me to focus on other potential trading setups that require watching the price action more closely.

Get It? Got It? Good!

- To be a pro, you have to approach trading as a business, not a hobby!
- Don't rely on luck; preparation is the key to good trading.
- Emotions can kill profits. Write out your trading plan to give your trades a fighting chance.
- Always know your loss limits. In the words of John Paulson, "Watch the downside, the upside will take care of itself."
- Make the exits just as sharp as entries.

Chapter Fourteen

Crash, Burn, and Learn

Becoming a Better Trader

WHEN MOST PEOPLE THINK OF BASKETBALL, they think of Michael Jordan, one of the best basketball players of all time. In 1999, he was named the greatest North American athlete of the twentieth century by the sports network ESPN. Ask almost anyone who follows sports and they will say that when it comes to playing basketball, Jordan is a raging success.

Yet the following quote is one of the most memorable things that Michael Jordan has ever said and hands down one of the best sports quotes I've heard.

———————————— ❧ ————————————

**I've missed more than 9,000 shots in my
career. I've lost almost 300 games. Twenty-six
times, I've been trusted to take the game-
winning shot and missed. I've failed over and
over and over again in my life. And that
is why I succeed.**

————————————————————————

Every good trader has crashed and burned and wiped
out a number of trading accounts before turning a consistent profit, and even then there will be losing streaks, but
as Michael Jordan suggested, failure is a critical part of
success. No matter how much thought we have put into
our trading plan and no matter how well we have analyzed
the data and charts, markets can trip us up and stop us
out at any given time. The important thing is to learn
from our mistakes because as Carl Jung, the father of
analytical psychology once said, "Knowledge rests not
upon truth alone, but upon error also."

How can we learn from our mistakes? In the last
chapter, we learned how to create a trading plan, but the
other piece of the puzzle is to keep a trading log. Start a
simple Excel spreadsheet with a running tally of your
trades, noting the currency pair that you traded, the strategy that you used (if there is one), the time that you

entered the trade, the price that you entered at, the stop, your profit or loss, and a column for special notes such as *"That was a bad trade! Should have avoided Fed meeting"* or *"Should have stayed in the trade longer!"* These notes to yourself will become extremely useful when you review your trades and find room for improvement.

Albert Einstein once said, "We can't solve problems by using the same kind of thinking we used when we created them." Regardless of whether I am on a winning or losing streak, every Sunday morning, after I have taken a break from the market and can look at it from a fresh perspective, I will bring up my Excel spreadsheet and look at the trades and my notes to see if there is any pattern worth noting. I don't forcibly look for patterns but have found that they are all the more obvious after a day of not looking at the charts.

Tracking your trades on an Excel spreadsheet is exceptionally useful because it allows you to sort the data by currency pair, time of day, and everything else to see if there are patterns in your success and failures. Hypothetically, for example, I may find that 80 percent of my long trades hit their profit targets while 70 percent of short trades were stopped out. This does not mean that I should immediately stop selling currency pairs and trade only to the long side. Instead, I would dig deeper into those trades to try to understand why this is happening.

Perhaps I am ignoring the overall trend in the market because all of the currency pairs have been in strong uptrends or there is simply no logical explanation for the losses. Either way it is worth a try because you never know what you will discover!

Like every other trader, I, too, have crashed, burned, and learned. Here are three of the major lessons that I have taken away and the changes that I made after reviewing my trades:

Lesson 1: Stick to Currencies with Smaller Spreads

In Chapter 8, we learned about many different ways to use the Double Bollinger Bands, and if you recall, one of those ways was to get into a new trend. With this specific strategy, positions are normally held for 1 to 12 hours and entered at the close of the New York trading session. Since this strategy looks for a continuation that can be large or small, I normally risk no more than 60 pips on the trade. In the early years when I first started to trade this setup, I would focus exclusively on the strategy. I would patiently wait for the setup to form across various currency pairs and when it occurred, I would apply the same stop and first target to all the positions.

However, I quickly realized that some trades were being stopped more often than others. When I initially noticed this pattern, I continued to trade because I wanted to gather a larger sample before making any changes to my trading strategy. One or two bad trades is not enough to change the entire trading plan. After taking 50 some-odd trades across different currency pairs, I sorted the transactions in an Excel spreadsheet and realized that I was stopped out in 5 out of 5 AUD/NZD trades and 3 out of 4 EUR/CAD trades. After some additional investigation, I realized that the spread in the currency pairs was killing my trades. The spread, which is the difference between the buy and sell price for AUD/NZD and EUR/CAD, could reach as much as 12 pips during the early Asian trading session, which was basically right after I put on my trade. This means that realistically my stop is only 48 and not 60 pips. Considering that the average daily trading range for both currency pairs is fairly wide, 48 pips is not that significant. Therefore, I found that those trades were frequently being stopped out on nothing more than market noise. Also spreads have a tendency of widening during the early Asian trading session when many U.S. traders have gone home for the day and Asian traders have yet to arrive at their offices.

In retrospect, I consider this an amateur mistake, but even professionals were amateurs at one point and had to learn how to be pros the hard way. From that time forward, I did not use the Double Bollinger Bands to get into a new trend in currency pairs with spreads wider than 6 pips. If my stop was larger, like 100 pips or so, I may have considered trading the wider spread pairs, but for this particular trading strategy, I will not.

Lesson 2: Use the Right Stop

In Lesson 1, I mentioned that I use a 60-pip stop when I use the Double Bollinger Bands to get into a new trend. However, I did not always use a 60-pip stop. In the past, I had a stop of 70 pips, which you may not consider to be all that different from a 60-pip stop, but every pip counts! Even when I am on a hot streak, hitting back-to-back winners, I still went back and reviewed my trades every week. On one rainy Sunday in 2005 when I had nothing better to do, I decided to look through my losing trades one by one on the charts to see if there was room for improvement. It was through this process that I realized when a trade went against me by more than 60 pips, it would be stopped 97 percent of the time.

Let's take a moment and think about what this means in more detail. With the Double Bollinger Band new trend strategy, we usually enter into the position when the currency pair has closed into the zone between the one and two standard deviation Double Bollinger Bands after trading within the range-trading zone, with the hope of joining a new trend. Therefore, if the currency pair moves 60 pips against us, then most likely it has moved out of the uptrend or downtrend zones and is back inside the range-trading zone, which means that it failed to form a new trend. Therefore, it really doesn't matter if it moved 60 or 70 pips because, either way, the reason for getting into the trade no longer holds. From that time forward, a stop of 60 pips has been the sweet spot for this strategy.

It was also through some serious review of my trades that I found my sweet spot for trailing stops. When it comes to using trailing stops, I always encourage traders to be creative and use a stop that fits their goals. Some people enter for a technical reason such as a break above a moving average and want to exit for the same reason. Other people cannot monitor their trades all the time and instead will use an automated trailing stop. With most of my trading strategies, after I hit the first target I like to use a stop of 30 pips and move it every 20 pips. The reason is that 30 pips gives the trade enough breathing room, so even if there is a retrace, it would need to be a fairly large one that is probably triggered by a news event or a change in short-term sentiment to stop me out. Moving it every 20 pips lets me keep a close lock on my profits, trailing it regularly as the momentum of the currency pair pushes it further in my favor. Just imagine that you are a marathon runner: There is only so far that you can fall behind before you know that you have lost the race.

Lesson 3: Pick the Right Time to Trade News

In Chapter 9, we learned how to trade news. One of the cardinal rules of this trading tactic is to wait five minutes before getting into the trade to avoid the initial volatility and to make sure that the market actually cares about the data. This too was another lesson that I learned through my years of trading and watching the market because if the data is significant enough, there will be continuation.

Another interesting observation has to do with the Canadian dollar's reaction to economic data. Unlike other currency pairs that will usually react the millisecond that the number is released, Canadian data tends to have a delayed reaction. For example, on August 11, 2010, Canada reported a trade deficit that was much wider than economists had anticipated. If it were any other currency pair, we would expect it to sell off immediately at 8:30 A.M. Eastern Time; however, the CAD did not. The Canadian dollar waited a full 10 minutes before suddenly breaking sharply lower against the U.S. dollar. Within four minutes, USD/CAD jumped from 1.0383 to a high of 1.0430, which is a fairly significant short-term move for the currency pair. Over the next three hours, USD/CAD climbed another

40 pips to a high of 1.0474. This type of delayed reaction is fairly typical for USD/CAD, but only traders who have stared at the currency for hours and hours would have discovered this behavior! Part of the reason this happens is Canadian data tends to be released at the same time as U.S. data and so forex traders want to see how the market responds to the U.S. data before they take a position in the Canadian dollar.

Occasionally, if I have a strong reason to believe that a piece of data will be good or bad, I will take a trade before the number is released. Usually I enter into the trade 20 minutes before the data is scheduled to be out. After thorough analysis of both winning and losing trades, I have found that 20 minutes is the sweet spot because it is generally short enough that the market is focusing almost exclusively on the economic release but long enough that spreads have not started to widen, which can happen 5 to 10 minutes before the data is released. This is important because we do not want to pay up for a currency pair simply because the spreads between the buy and sell price have increased.

The addition of the 50-period SMA has also come out of this review process. In the past I found that when the sentiment in the market runs counter to the surprise in the data, the chance that the trade will hit the profit target is smaller unless it is a major surprise in a very important economic release. The addition of the SMA has helped to filter out the weaker trades that are not supported by the general market sentiment.

A Warning about Fitting to Perfection

There are many things that you can learn from conducting your own review process and making enhancements to your trading. The trick is to not fit to perfection by making changes in reaction to bad trades. Only make changes that make sense after a statistically significant number of trades (which means a lot of them)!

Pick a quiet day when you are not trading to sit back and think about things rationally and see if there is room for improvement. If you can't do it every week, do it at least once a month. Some of the things that you may want to consider when reviewing your trades include the time of day that you are trading, the impact of holding positions overnight and over the weekend, and the currency pairs that you have chosen to trade. Also consider whether you are cutting your winning trades too quickly or holding onto your losing trades for too long. We can all benefit from self-reflection and self-improvement. As Oliver Cromwell, the English military and political leader, once said, "He who stops being better stops being good."

Get It? Got It? Good!

- Keep a log of all your trades so you can see what you are doing right and wrong.
- Set aside a regular time to review your trading log and look for patterns. You'll be surprised how the log will shine a spotlight on your successes or mistakes!
- Write notes to yourself as reminders about things to avoid, such as trading non-farm payrolls or holding positions when there is a G20 meeting over the weekend.
- Don't change your trading strategy just because you had one bad trade; make sure you have a good number of samples before making a change.
- Finally, only make enhancements to your trading that make logical sense!

Chapter Fifteen

Start Smart

Begin Your Currency Adventure the Right Way

THE NEXT TIME YOU VISIT DISNEY WORLD and meander through the World Showcase, think about how wonderful it is to experience different cultures. In this global day and age, it's common to have coworkers and clients in other countries. One of the great things about the Internet is that we can e-mail, chat, or call anyone in the world with the click of a button.

The world is really a very small place that is closely linked together. So goes the theory behind six degrees of separation. The idea is that every person is no more than six steps away from another person. For example, I know that I am no more than five and possibly only four degrees of separation from President Obama, and from him I am six degrees apart from every other major head of state. Isn't that exciting?

Unless you work for a brick-and-mortar company, there's a good chance that you have clients or vendors outside of your own country; if that's the case, then currencies are part of your life already. If this is not applicable, then it should only be a matter of time before you end up ordering or selling something to someone in another country. People around the world have done and will continue to do business with each other. In places such as Germany and Singapore, investors are even more aware of currency movements because they rely heavily on imports and exports to other countries. Many Singaporeans have children studying abroad in the United Kingdom, Australia, and the United States and so they are extremely sensitive to the ups and downs of exchange rates. The United States, on the other hand, is a very self-sufficient country with only approximately 30 percent of Americans owning a passport compared to approximately 70 percent in the United Kingdom. This trend has changed and will continue to change as more Americans open their eyes to the opportunities beyond U.S. borders. As a result, many investors in the United States have already incorporated currencies as part of their trading and investment strategies. They realize that currencies and exchange rates will be part of our lives forever.

The times are changing and you have a choice to either ignore it and be left behind or adapt to it. Remember the statistic provided by the Bank of International Settlements that shows foreign exchange volume doubling between 2003 and 2010? A good part of this increase in volume can be credited to the participation of individual investors. Although investment institutions and other professional investors have been trading currencies for decades, it is still a relatively new market for individuals.

As you have learned from this book, there are many ways to access the foreign exchange market; between now and the next 10 years, the number of instruments will probably increase even further. Regulators around the world have taken steps to make the market safer for investors and, as a result, we will probably see more people trade forex.

What the bursting of the technology bubble, the global financial crisis, and the European debt crisis should have taught all of us is that financial disasters repeat themselves—their shapes and sizes may be different but the consequences for most investors are always the same. When disaster strikes again, you have the option of watching portfolio values evaporate or getting in control. One of the secrets of success in life is to be ready to grab opportunities when they arise. Get ahead of the curve by learning how the market works, how to manage its unique risks, and how to trade it today.

It doesn't take a disaster to create opportunities in the forex market. If the global economy starts to recover and enters a phase of growth, there could be a string of positive surprises in economic data. This could also offer opportunities for traders—just as currencies can reflect to pessimism, they will also reflect their optimism.

Thankfully, there is a tremendous amount of free forex education and research provided by independent companies and forex brokers. Take advantage of them! Take your time; there is no need to rush into forex trading. The forex market has been around for a very long time and will continue to remain active for decades to come, so take your time to really learn about how the market works before you place your first trade.

As Benjamin Franklin once said, "Energy and persistence conquers all things"; as long as you are willing to approach forex trading with the seriousness and the discipline of a business, you are ready to tread ahead confidently. Knowledge of the market, a good strategy, solid money management, and a little bit of luck will go a long way.

Author's Disclaimer

⸺⸺⸺⸺⸺⸺⸺⸺ ∾ ⸺⸺⸺⸺⸺⸺⸺⸺

Forex (and futures) trading involves high risks, with the potential for substantial losses and is not suitable for all people. Past performance is not indicative of future results. Any opinions, news, research, analyses, prices, or other information contained in this book is provided as general market commentary, and does not constitute investment advice. Kathy Lien is not liable for any loss or damage, including, without limitation, any loss of profit that may arise directly or indirectly from use of or reliance on such information. As the markets evolve, the content of this book is subject to change at any time without notice and is provided for the sole purpose of assisting traders to make independent investment decisions. Kathy Lien has taken reasonable measures to ensure the accuracy of the information in the book. At the time of publication, Lien was employed as co-head of global research for Global Forex Trading, a division of Global Futures & Forex, Ltd. (GFT). However, this book was written separately and independently from her employment with GFT. GFT does not control the content of the book, and opinions expressed by Lien are not necessarily those of GFT.